Young Christians in Russia

YOUNG CHRISTIANS
IN RUSSIA

Michael Bourdeaux
and
Katharine Murray

LAKELAND
MARSHALL MORGAN & SCOTT
116 Baker Street
LONDON W1M 2BB

KESTON BOOKS No. 5

Printed in Great Britain by
Cox & Wyman Ltd,
London, Reading and Fakenham

Contents

Acknowledgements

Grateful thanks to the research staff of Keston College (the Centre for the Study of Religion and Communism), and especially Kathy Matchett, for their help and guidance in the collection of material for this book. Also to Michael Harris for secretarial help. Above all, thanks to David Murray for his encouragement and for doing without his wife's company for many long evenings during the final stages of editing.

This book is in a very real sense a product of the teamwork which is part of the everyday life of Keston College. My own thanks are due especially to Katharine Murray, because she has contributed far more to the book at all stages than I have.

MICHAEL BOURDEAUX

Introduction

GO, ON A sunny spring day, to the heart of the USSR, to Red Square in the centre of Moscow. Follow the long queue which stretches from the door of a square red-marble building under the Kremlin walls. Take your turn to enter the door of Lenin's mausoleum, descend the steps out of the cheerful sunlight into the gloom, where the waxy, yellow features of a long-dead leader are lit eerily in the surrounding twilight. The crowds shuffle past silently, reverently—old men and young teachers with parties of schoolchildren, Easterners in embroidered caps, and foreign tourists. All these come to pay their respects to the father of the Russian revolution and of the modern Soviet state.

Then come out, blinking, into the brightness, and read the slogans blazoned on the buildings around: 'Lenin lives!'; 'The spirit of Lenin is in the hearts of the Soviet people!' Then perhaps you will understand a little of what it is that is leading many of the new Soviet generation to worship the living Christ. In spite of an upbringing and an education which denies His very existence, in spite of the alienation from a secular society which becoming a believer entails, there are young Christians in Russia.

Communism has been called a religion, but it is less than that. True, an individual may devote himself to its service, but in the end all he is serving is the impersonal State who cares little for him. In the early days, and even to some extent still today, young people in the USSR could throw their enthusiasm into the building of a new life and a new future. But for most of them the new future has not turned out as they had expected. Ideals have been abandoned. The Soviet Union is now merely following the West on the road of materialism—better technology and more consumer goods, a new home for everyone and holidays by the Black Sea. Small wonder there is a craving for higher goals than these. Atheist articles in the press have remarked that what young people are looking for most of all is a meaning to life. 'Religion,' wrote a Leningrad school-leaver in reply to a questionnaire, 'gives the believer some hope in life. He believes in something, mythical though it may be, for a person cannot live without faith.' (*Questions of Scientific Atheism,* vol. 9 (1970) p. 60.)

It is only a step from the mausoleum of Lenin to the architectural glories of St Basil's Cathedral. Turn the corner from Red Square and you will find yourself in a street filled with little churches, each one a gem of its own kind, taking one back into the Russia of the past. Here is a path that some of the new generation of Russians are taking, away from the drabness of the present. The art, the music, the architecture of pre-revolutionary days holds a powerful fascination for them, helping them to find their identity in a nation whose traditions have been pulled up by the roots. Much of this heritage is Christian. The mediaeval icon painters, the beautiful intricacies of Orthodox church music —both their rich colourfulness and their deep religious meaning are wholly different from the Soviet world. Here is a heritage through which God may speak—and is speaking— to some of the new generation. For some it may be no more than a fashionable rebelliousness, but for others it is a pathway to 'the unspeakable riches of Christ'.

The following pages present something of the story of those for whom the vacuum in Soviet life has been filled by the love of God. They are the future of the Church in the Soviet Union. Have they something to say to the Church in the West? I think you will find that they have.

1 / Young Christians and the future of the Church

'ON 8 NOVEMBER 1971 a group of Christian children and young people aged between twelve and fifteen were on the local train on their way home from an evening meeting. They were accompanied by an older girl whose father is in prison, and by the mother of one of the boys. It was ten o'clock in the evening. The girl had a guitar with her and the boys were reading from the Gospels.

'Suddenly two young men entered the compartment. They sat down near the girl and asked her to play a popular song on her guitar. She replied: "I don't play that kind of song." "Then play whatever you can," they said. At their request she sang them a Christian song.

'These young men, it turned out, were agents-provocateurs. One of them, after listening to the song, stood up and said to the other, "I'm off now . . ." The other stayed in the compartment. A few minutes later two policemen came in.

'The boys hid the Gospels behind their backs when they saw the policemen. One of them went up to the boys and asked: "What's that you're reading? Let me see it." He took the Gospel from the children. Then he demanded that they hand over all the religious literature they had, and began to search the children.

'One of the boys asked, "Have you got a search warrant?"

' "We'll take you off to the station and there we'll have a warrant for your arrest and all."

'In spite of the protests of the mother and the girl, and of the children themselves, he confiscated all their notebooks full of hymns and poems. Then, to cries from one or two atheists on the train, "All the Baptists ought to be shot for corrupting children like that!" the policemen and their helpers took the children to the office of the railway police. There they were questioned about where they had been and who had preached about Christ. The children did not answer these questions. Seeing they would find out nothing, the police kept them until two o'clock in the morning and then let them go ... The city transport had stopped running. The children, scared by the thought of being shot, upset by the confiscation of their Gospels and poetry, reached home late at night where their parents were waiting for them in alarm.'

□

The above extract is from the Reform Baptists' clandestine journal *Herald of Salvation*, no. 1, 1972. It takes a lot of courage for a child or young person openly to profess faith in Christ in the Soviet Union today. Yet this group of young Baptists is not alone. All the evidence suggests that, in spite of the pressures, large numbers of the younger generation are not afraid to call themselves Christians. Even the Soviet press, hostile to religion in all its forms, admits that this is true.

Before the revolution of 1917, few children, in Western Russia at least, grew up ignorant of the basic doctrines of Christianity. The educational system was dominated by the Russian Orthodox Church. It was Lenin's Bolshevik government which abolished religious instruction in schools, and instituted instead compulsory instruction in a secular world-view. Following the aims of the Communist party, the new generation were to become leaders in militant atheism. They were to set an example and teach their elders to abandon the old ways. Religion was declared to be a relic of the barbarous past. It was a means by which social injustice had been perpetuated, and had no place in the society of the future. The New Soviet Man was to have no corner of his heart devoted to the God of his fathers.

In 1918, the *Decree on the Separation of the School from*

the Church forbade the Church to organise its own courses of instruction for children. Outside the privacy of the family circle all teaching of Christianity was thus effectively ended. All this is nearly sixty years ago. The younger generation—like the two generations before it—is growing up in a secular, atheist atmosphere. Human effort alone is presented as the way to achieve Heaven on earth, the ultimate goal of true Communism. Educated man, say the atheists, is able to see just how irrational religious faith is. The few churches which remain are only tolerated in order to keep the old people happy. Let the last few die, and religion will vanish from the face of Russia. This is the theme of the propagandists.

A book on the atheist education of children—*Children and Religion*, by I. I. Ogryzko, published in Leningrad in 1970—has this to say about the beliefs of young people (p. 5):

☐

'In 1966–67 the Department of Scientific Atheism of the Herzen Pedagogical Institute in Leningrad carried out a sociological survey in Leningrad schools on the subject, "The effectiveness of atheist education in schools". 1,619 pupils in the final year were questioned in twenty-eight different schools. Each one filled in a questionnaire, and 1,134 of them wrote an essay on the subject, "My attitude to religion". Anonymity was maintained throughout to ensure the maximum of openness.

'The results of the survey showed that amongst final year students in Leningrad the proportion which is completely free from religious ideas is about 97 per cent. The Soviet school, family and society can be proud of this success in atheist education amongst the rising generation.'

☐

All this sounds like bad news for the Churches. Soviet statistics, however, do not always tell the whole story. In general the policy of Soviet publishing and the press is not merely to report, but to exhort and encourage towards the State's chosen goals. Careful selection can achieve this. Successes for the atheist cause are more likely to be mentioned than failures. Furthermore, those who fill in questionnaires for the researchers do not necessarily have much faith in their 'anonymity'.

Nevertheless, official sources have their story to tell. The fact that they mention Christian young people at all reveals that they are more concerned about their numbers than they dare to say. This extract is from the Lithuanian journal *The Communist* (September 1973, p. 62):

☐

'We must not be lulled into complacency by the fact that atheism is winning the battle against religion. The fact remains that a small proportion of young people who have spent eleven years in a Soviet school, and have learnt the basic precepts of both natural and social science, are still, to a greater or lesser extent, under the influence of religion.'

☐

Against admissions like this, not uncommon in atheist writings, must be placed enthusiastic reports from different parts of the Church, telling of a great upsurge of interest in Christianity among young people. The evidence, from both sources, is fragmentary. No-one has ever done a survey to find out exactly how many of the young generation are followers of Christ. Nobody knows with certainty how typical are the isolated instances of which we have detailed information. The USSR is vast and varied, and what is true in Lithuania cannot necessarily be applied in Vladivostok. But let us look at the pieces of the puzzle and see if they fall into a coherent pattern.

We have seen what the authorities will admit about the proportion of young people in the churches. Now let us look at the experience of an Orthodox priest from Moscow, Father Dmitri Dudko. This conversation was held on 28 July 1972, in the office of the Moscow Procuracy, the chief legal authority for the district:

☐

'Q. Why are there so many young people around you?
A. (smiling) I love young people . . . With young people, you get younger yourself . . .

14

Q. But what are you indoctrinating them with? Are you putting slanderous thoughts into their heads?

A. I talk to them on religious topics.

Q. In the churches it's 90 per cent old people. Of course they won't argue with you . . .

A. You're behind the times. Many young people go to church now. You should be grateful to me that I keep young people away from crime . . . People have a thirst for religion now. I'll tell you about one case. The son of a highly-placed man, a secret policeman, Party member for seventeen years, he makes his confessions with me, a deeply religious person . . . His father wanted to give me what for, but when he came and spoke to me, he realised that I was having a good influence on his son who was tending to drink. He invited me to his home, I put his son's family life in order. When the son left the room, the father bowed to me and said: "Thank you, you're a good influence on my son, he's even stopped cursing Communists". Young people are interested in religious questions.

Q. But only because you're indoctrinating them . . .

A. You can't indoctrinate with religion. I don't like proofs. I mean I'm not against them . . . But you can't indoctrinate people with religion, you have to feel it. Young people are beginning to feel it. In twelve years I have already baptised about 1,000 adults. And I know how they came to accept God . . . The main weakness of atheist propaganda is that it tries to indoctrinate . . . So it's produced a reverse reaction. Everyone has become fed up with atheism. No-one reads atheist literature . . .'

☐

The Churches—the last bastion of a dying generation? Even the atheist literature has at times to admit that this is not so. The monthly magazine *Science and Religion* is devoted to atheist education, but sometimes it too reveals just how strong is the Church's influence on the young. This article appeared in the issue of September 1966, pp. 73–5.

15

The writer is on a visit to Odessa which happens to fall on Easter eve. First he visits a Catholic church:

□

'Three little girls, about twelve or thirteen years old, with bulging school bags, crossed the gardens and stopped by a large stone pedestal opposite the church. One of them—a skinny little thing with a thick plait of hair—jumped up and pointed: "There they are!"

'Three women, opening their bags as they walked, briskly approached the girls. With a jealous look at her friends' daughters, each one began to untie the Pioneer scarf on the neck of her own child, shoved it into her bag, pulled a little cross on a chain out of her purse and put it round the girl's neck. The mothers picked up the briefcases, and all six hurried towards the church. In a second they had disappeared through the doors. A minute more and I followed them.

'The solemn mass had just begun. Believers were still coming in through the doors. Quite a few were youths and girls. Each one, lowering his eyes, would place a coin in the box, dip his fingers in the marble bowl of holy water, put his lips to the crucifix, genuflect, and then go to stand behind the rows of seats. All the seats were already full.

'Where were the little Pioneers? I looked around the church for the tenth time. In the front row children were kneeling: five boys and three girls. All were about six or seven years old. They attentively followed the priest's movements as he changed from one set of vestments into another, each more splendid than the last. Then the sermon began . . .'

Next the reporter visits the Baptist church:

'My next port of call was 34 Serov Street. This was the prayer-house of the Evangelical Christians and Baptists. Outside the evening was cool, but inside it was stuffy, hot, the air close and stifling. On the wall there was a crude painting of a landscape (a fairy-tale valley with ice-covered

16

cliffs). Above was the text "God is love" in ornate lettering. Believers were sitting on benches. Here too there were young people, children. Pale, perspiring little faces of children. A moustached pastor stood in the pulpit.

'Suddenly an old woman with an hysterical look jumped to her feet and shouted violently, "Praise Him, praise the Lord, our Saviour! Praise Him, praise Him, praise Him!"

'The pastor stopped in mid-syllable and the congregation began to pray fervently. A little girl in a red jacket sitting just in front of me intoned earnestly, "Lo-o-rd, our Saviour and the Saviour of all Christians ..." '

Then the writer calls on the headmistress of one of the local schools, and asks how they are going about the re-education of all these believing children. 'Believing children?' is the indignant reply, 'We don't have any.'

Finally he interviews the local police chief, who tells him the following story. It so happens that that year the celebration of the liberation of Odessa during the last war fell on the same day as Easter:

'A relative of mine teaches in the primary school at Arkady—just outside Odessa. All week she talked to the children in practically every lesson about the heroic defence of Odessa and how the city had been liberated from the Fascist invaders. Today she asked them, "Children, what day is it tomorrow?" With one voice the children replied "Easter!" That means there must have been a great deal of talk at home about the coming festival.'

☐

Here is the atheist press itself, admitting that the old myth that the Church only attracts old people simply does not hold water. A new generation is growing up in the churches which holds fast to its faith in spite of the secularism all around. Child baptisms and church marriages of young people are common—and this disturbs the authorities. There may be other motives, apart from the purely religious one, for wanting such ceremonies. The substitutes provided

17

by the State are not always popular. For instance, a couple wanting to get married, if they desire more than a drab ten minutes in a registry office, may have to travel some way to the nearest town to a 'Palace of Happiness', where ceremonial weddings can be arranged. When they get there they may find themselves in a queue of couples waiting for the ceremonial treatment. And the arrangements themselves are often disappointing. In an amusing article in the youth paper *Komsomol Truth* on 14 June 1973, a young man complains that he and his bride have decided not to go through with the ceremony after all. In an attempt to make it colourful and attractive, his Ukrainian 'Palace of Happiness' has dug out a number of old national customs, long since abandoned by the people. Why, asks this bridegroom, should they be forced to go to the expense of buying the traditional Ukrainian *rushnik*—a type of embroidered towel—just so that they can stand on it during the ceremony? He finds the whole thing ridiculous and would prefer to be able to arrange his own form of service.

Small wonder, then, that some young couples decide that the dignity of a traditional church service is more acceptable, on purely aesthetic grounds. The atheist establishment views even this with some disquietude. They consider the provision of suitable ceremonies to mark the significant moments of life to be an important element in weaning people away from the influence of the Church.

One young couple, who decided to marry in the cathedral of St Vladimir in Kiev, were severely criticised in the press. The wedding took place in 1970, and the couple in question were both members of the Komsomol, the Communist youth movement. They made no secret of their intentions, invited their friends, and were even praised by some for their act of boldness. The pair declared that the decision to marry in church had nothing to do with their beliefs, and that they were, in fact, atheists. They just did it 'for a lark'.

Others, however, have more genuine motives. The annual volume published for the use of atheist activists,

Questions of Scientific Atheism (vol. 9, 1970, p. 65), has this to say:

☐

'A survey of young believers has shown that the underlying reason for the conclusion of religious marriages is not only the beauty and sense of joyful celebration in the ceremony, but the hope that the church wedding itself will bring about a united family . . .'

☐

The baptism of young babies is also widespread amongst young couples, although the press asserts that in most cases it is done on the insistence of grandmothers and other older relatives. Sometimes both the civil and religious ceremonies are asked for. Percentages for baptisms given in the press are generally high. The magazine *Agitator* (December 1966, p. 42) reports that in the Vyborg district of Leningrad 37 per cent of children are baptised. Surveys carried out in industry and published in *Questions of Scientific Atheism* in 1970 (p. 196) report 50 per cent. An interesting breakdown of figures for the city of Gorky is given in *Young Communist* (November 1969, p. 95): 60 per cent of parents having their children baptised are under thirty, and 67 per cent have above average education. 20 per cent are Komsomol members. As to their attitudes to Christianity, only 3·5 per cent declared themselves to be believers. 10 per cent called themselves 'undecided', 26 per cent atheists, and the remainder, 60·5 per cent, simply 'unbelievers'. 25 per cent only, however, said that they were totally unaware of the ceremony's religious significance and regarded it purely as an old Russian custom.

As with all statistics, there may be more in these than meets the eye. One must bear in mind that a price may have to be paid for the baptism of one's child. A young father was recently refused membership of the Communist party because his child had been baptised, despite his assertion that it had been done at his wife's insistence and without his knowledge. This was reported in *Komsomol Truth* for 25 August 1971. A recent ruling that the parents' documents must be presented before the child can be baptised (supposedly to prevent the 'kidnapping' of a child by older relatives against the parents' will), means that every parent is identified and recorded by name if he goes through with the ceremony. Those couples who were questioned may have been reluctant to state their true beliefs.

In the predominantly Lutheran Baltic republics of Latvia and Estonia, the confirmation of children in their teens was a general practice before the Soviet takeover in 1939. To compete with the Lutherans the Orthodox Church there also introduced a coming-of-age ceremony (whereas normally the laying-on of hands follows immediately on infant baptism). In 1957, 49 per cent of all eighteen-year-olds in Estonia came forward for confirmation. This was no mere formality. A considerable amount of preparation preceded it. Often the young people would live together at the pastorate for three weeks beforehand for a period of intensive instruction. In 1957, however, a civil coming-of-age ceremony was introduced to draw young people away from the Church. About a third of the young people in the age-group were successfully drawn into it. However, despite the pressure to do otherwise, at least two thousand young people each year—about 10 per cent—are still being confirmed. This is the figure given by the head of the Lutheran Church in a talk on Danish radio in August 1969, and does not include Orthodox figures. He was speaking with the express permission of the authorities and obviously no mention could be made of confirmations which may be carried out in secret. Even so, the numbers are quite large.

From these facts a picture is beginning to emerge, and it is certainly not the one which Lenin envisaged at the time of the Revolution. A young generation growing up with the education to enlighten their elders? Perhaps this is true in some cases, if the atheist propaganda is to be believed. But in 1976, 59 years after the Bolshevik revolution, an undercurrent of religious belief still flows strongly amongst the younger generation. Churches and believers are not scorned, but children are taken to worship with their elders. As they grow up, young people still prefer religious rather than civil ceremonies for their marriages and the baptism of their children. All this in the third generation to grow up under Communist secularism and be educated in the 'scientific atheism' of the school curriculum.

One final example of this fact. In Lithuania, which was not annexed by the Soviet Union until 1939, the Roman Catholic Church claims the allegiance of most of the population. In recent years there has been particular pressure on believers in Lithuania, following massive protests against the limitations imposed on the church. Children and young people especially are liable to be discriminated against if they are known to be believers. They may be publicly shamed before their schoolmates, or mocked in the wall newspapers which are a feature of Soviet school life. But children may be well able to defend their beliefs, and they do receive support from their classmates. This is what happened to one such child. The story is told in the *Chronicle of the Lithuanian Catholic Church* (no. 5, February 1973).

☐

'In April 1972, Lina Galinskaite, a tenth-grade student at the High School of Astrioji Kirsna, knelt down to pray at the funeral of a neighbour. The High School Professional Committee Chairman and the local Party Secretary became very indignant over the action. Lina was publicly criticised "for kneeling and blessing herself" by her class teacher at a specially convened emergency class meeting the following day.

' "I knelt, and I will continue to kneel. I blessed myself, and will continue to do so. You won't prohibit it because you haven't the right," the brave girl retorted.

' "You can crawl around if you want to," came the reply, "but you will pay for it either by being dismissed from the school or by receiving a failure mark in conduct."

'The two officials decided to put the case of the young girl before the entire student body. They felt that the Komsomol members would condemn her.

' "We pray in church ourselves," replied the students

21

when they heard the charge. "How can we condemn her?"

'The Trade Union committee chairman called a meeting of the production staff in the hope that at least the cleaning women would agree to condemn the girl. The women spoke up in defence of the student.'

☐

Such solidarity must indeed be rare, certainly outside Lithuania, where faithfulness to the Church is closely linked with a fierce nationalism and anti-Russian feeling. However it is a far cry from the 'small proportion of young people ... more or less under the influence of religion' claimed by the atheist writer quoted on p. 14 in his article about Lithuanian schools.

So far, much of what we have seen could be termed evidence of the *survival* of Christianity in an atheist state. Each generation has succeeded in passing on some of its own experience and beliefs to the following one. There is no greater influence on a child than that of its own family, and many of the young people in the Churches today have been brought up in Christian homes. Atheist statistics claim, indeed, that 85–90 per cent of believers are brought into the Church through relatives—either their parents or other members of the family. Grandmothers have a much stronger influence than in many Western countries. Children whose mothers go out to work are often brought up by the grandmother who lives with the family. The State's aim is that such children should be cared for in day-nurseries, but these are not nearly universal yet. So even where a child's parents are not believers, a deeply religious grandmother may pass on her faith. Many an Orthodox grandmother will insist on a child being baptised before she consents to look after it. There will be plenty of opportunities for her to instil some Christian teaching at the most impressionable age.

So Christianity survives. But further—is there any evidence of its *revival* among the younger generation? Are young people becoming Christians from completely secular backgrounds? The Soviet press is reluctant to report instances which suggest that this is so, but sometimes it cannot avoid it. What disturbs atheist militants most is that they see young people coming into the Church from outside who are very far indeed from their stereotype of a believer. Ignorant, superstitious, poorly educated and utterly unquestioning in his acceptance of dogma—this is the image which for years the press has portrayed of the average Christian. Now they have to admit that there is a 'new' kind of believer, who may be highly educated, firmly convinced and well able to defend himself in rational argument.

In August 1973, the youth paper *Komsomol Truth* published a series of three articles about a young man called Ivan Sidorenko (9, 24 and 25 August). Ivan had been known as a keen Komsomol member, a conscientious worker, a gregarious character who was the life and soul of every party. Suddenly his face is missing from his old haunts, and his friends discover to their astonishment that he has been converted to Christianity. He is more likely to be found in the Baptist church than at drinking parties. The writer of the article, an atheist worker, pays him a visit—but retires in confusion, out-argued by the new convert. Ivan is unshakeable in his convictions. 'God revealed Himself to me' is an argument to which there is no answer.

Reflecting on the situation, the author comes to the conclusion that the evangelistic activities of the Baptists are outdoing the atheists' own propaganda:

☐

'Baptist pastors insist that every member of the Church must "actively labour for the Harvest-field of God, seek out lost souls and cleanse them from their stains". This is one of the conditions of "salvation". The subtlety of the phrasing with which the journal *Fraternal Herald*[1] appeals to its readers is remarkable—"spread the powerful fragrance of

[1] *Fraternal Herald* (Bratsky Vestnik) is the permitted publication of the organisation of registered Baptist churches (the All-Union Council of Evangelical Christian and Baptist Churches). The 'schismatic', or Reform Baptists as they are often known, have no officially-tolerated publications and few registered and thus legally operating churches.

Christ amongst those around us"—but the missionary, propagandistic meaning of this call is obvious . . .

'The schismatic Baptists are especially zealous to reach young people. If they fail, the congregations will only grow older. In Nikolaev one Georgi Zh.[1] was involved with enviable zeal in the recruitment of young people into the schismatic group. He went in search of like-minded people in the towns and villages of the region, giving them "homemade" literature. He taught "spiritual asceticism" in its most extreme form. "Do not love the world, nor what is in the world"—and this meant refusing to become involved in any social activities.

'The local schismatics have a youth choir and orchestra, and seek by every means to attract people. They lay on buses for their visitors, post notices about "concerts". They are anxious to open a Bible school too.

'But these are enough facts. They tell us unequivocally that the Baptist faith is alive, active, and ingenious in its fishing for souls . . .

'It would be false to assume that today the old methods of atheist propaganda work as unfailingly as they did. Some young believers today have eight or ten years of education under their belts. Their motives for turning to faith are complex. It is not always the fault of a religious family. As, for instance, in the story of Ivan Sidorenko . . .'

□

There are many more mentions in the Soviet press in recent years which show how much they are concerned that the numbers of young people in the churches are growing. Not only do those from Christian families remain faithful to their upbringing, but complete outsiders are coming in too. In the learned journal *Scientific Studies in Higher Education* (*Philosophy section*) (no. 3, 1973) the writer I. M. Yermakov says that the religious beliefs of the younger generation are definitely a 'new' form of faith. No longer, he states, are

---

[1] Almost certainly G. Zheltonozhko, who was tried in January 1972 in Nikolaev for the distribution of religious literature. He was sentenced to three years in a prison camp.

young people Christians just through ignorance and tradition, but instead they have a clear understanding of what it is that they believe.

On 23 November 1971, the *Teachers' Gazette* complained that children from atheist backgrounds as well as believing ones are becoming Christians. The Ukrainian paper *Soviet Culture* of 21 August 1968 states that the number of young people joining churches in the Ukraine is actually on the increase. *Science and Religion* (June 1972, p. 11), reporting on the failure to re-educate Baptist children in the spirit of atheism, remarks that this is a matter of national concern. On 12 March 1970 the *Literary Gazette* recounted the experience of a young atheist teacher in a village where the *majority* of children go to church, whether Baptist or Orthodox. *Youth of Estonia* (23 August 1972) observed in amazement the entry of a young physics graduate into the Orthodox theological seminary in Leningrad—and this is one of many such reports.

As usual, what the Soviet press lets slip in brief asides, the churches themselves assert in ringing tones. The testimony of the Orthodox priest quoted on pp. 14–15 speaks for itself. Numbers of Russian Protestants of German descent have left the Soviet Union in recent years. All their leaders testify to the lively faith among young people in the USSR. But many of them have expressed disillusion with what they feel to be the coldness and indifference to Christian ideals by young Christians in the West. Pastor Arnold Rose, who left the Soviet Union to live in West Germany in 1971, said in an interview on Norwegian television in December 1973 that a revival was going on in the unofficial Baptist Church which was largely touching young people. No such assertion comes from the registered Baptists, but owing to the stringent restrictions placed by the State on youth work, it would not be in their interests to publicise the state of affairs. Unlike the unofficial wing of the Church, they have much to lose.

This is no more than an outline sketch of young Christians in Russia today. The real picture is complex and detailed, built up from the miniscule brush-strokes of the experience of individuals. A picture which for us who observe from a distance is blurred, incomplete, and often distorted through the lens of a prejudiced atheist eye. The rest of this book is devoted to the experience of those individuals who have come sharply into focus for us in the West, because their own writings, or writings about them, have filtered across the borders of the Soviet Union. Mikhail Meerson-Aksyonov and Yevgeni Barabanov, Orthodox Christians and deeply thoughtful intellectuals; Ivan Moiseyev, whose simple visionary faith brought him to a horrible, yet inspiring end; the Lithuanian Catholic youngsters who long to see Christian government in Soviet Lithuania. These, and many more—just a fragment of the life of the Church in the Soviet Union, where Christ lives on in the hearts of—who knows how many?—young people.

THE OUTSIDER, especially if he is a Westerner and a Protestant, might be forgiven for finding the idea of Soviet youngsters joining the Russian Orthodox Church a little anachronistic. Bejewelled icons, bearded priests, liturgy in a long-dead tongue, all these make the tourist who steps into an Orthodox church feel as if he has stepped back into the Middle Ages. What possible relevance can all this have to the younger generation of a country advancing towards Communism?

The Orthodox Church is still by far the largest in the Soviet Union, numbering at least ten million people. Historically the established church of Russia, its influence runs deep in the Russian consciousness. When they think of Christianity, it is to the Orthodox Church that Soviet people automatically turn.

However, its historical role has given the Church problems too. Mikhail Meerson-Aksyonov's *The People of God and the Pastors* (see next chapter) goes into these problems in depth. After centuries of close identification with the Tsarist régime, the revolution of 1917 left the Orthodox Church in search of a new method of entering into the way of life of the people. Though still hesitant, it is beginning, chiefly through its laity and parish clergy, to find a new consciousness. There has been an influx of thoughtful young people, the new intelligentsia, into the Orthodox Church, who are searching for a truly Christian way of life through the traditional forms. At the same time they are deeply concerned about social, moral and political issues, about art and culture. Far from retreating into a mediaeval world, some of them—albeit a minority—are active in the struggle for human rights, following in the footsteps of older Christians such as Alexander Solzhenitsyn and Anatoli Levitin. Andrei Tverdokhlebov, a young Orthodox Christian from Moscow, was founder-secretary of the first branch of Amnesty International ever to be formed in a Communist country. He was arrested on 18 April 1975 for his activities. Yevgeni Barabanov, whose story is told on pp. 41–46, was involved in the publication in the West of works of literature suppressed by Soviet censorship. He too is an Orthodox Christian.

Another young Orthodox wrote about the new movement in the Church in a letter written in 1969 to the *Messenger of the Russian Student Christian Movement*, published in Paris (English translation from *Sobornost*, vol. 5, no. 9). He describes what is happening amongst young Orthodox Christians as a 'religious renaissance':

□

'. . . In Russia we see the beginnings of an awakening from half a century of deep, nightmarish slumber. Today the age-old problems of life—the problems of God, of good and evil, of death, the building of a just society, etc.—are once again confronting the Russian consciousness, which has grown tired of idolatry. That is to say, the question is arising of a new consciousness, which must be Christian not only in part, or in its own separate sphere, but Christian in its totality . . .

'The Russian religious renaissance, which can be seen above all in the mood of the young intelligentsia, is a strong, spontaneous movement. We have no means of printing anything, no freedom of assembly, no free religious preaching, no guidance from the clergy, and finally, no books. But we have something else: the growing influx of a new ebullient force into Orthodoxy.'

□

This young writer speaks of a movement that has 'no guidance from the clergy'. Strong though the lay element may be, however, it is certainly not ignored by all the Orthodox clergy. The upper echelons of the hierarchy may not recognise it, at any rate not in its public pronouncements, for fear of attracting the attention of the State to the defection of its youth from official ideology. But on a parish level there are priests who lead and encourage young people in their search for truth. On 16 November 1970 *Komsomol Truth*, the newspaper of the communist youth movement, published the following account of a certain Moscow church which had become a centre for young believers:

☐

' "In Moscow there is a church," writes a certain Moscow student, "where educated and intelligent people often gather: students, musicians, artists. Here one can breathe the atmosphere of days gone by, relax after work, take part in interesting discussions, hear excellent performances of Bach, Rachmaninov or Chesnokov".

'The writer enthusiastically describes her impressions: "An unassuming-looking preacher amazed me by his erudition. He began his sermon with Marx, quoted Lenin. And you know, although I consider myself a militant atheist, one phrase has been imprinted involuntarily on my memory: "if even one of you who has come into this church has been made to think, we shall rejoice that our prayers have been heard by God".'

☐

Far from having lost touch with the everyday reality of Soviet life, the Orthodox Church is evidently very much in tune with the intellectual climate among young people. Certainly a deep impression was made on this atheist young girl. Here again are evidences of the 'new' type of Christian mentioned in the last chapter, who is better informed in his beliefs than the well-indoctrinated atheist.

The priesthood too is receiving its influx of young men, through which it is continually being renewed. For those who wish to train for the ministry—and there is no shortage of them—the way is not always easy. Theological education is strictly limited. During graduation week at Zagorsk in June 1974, Archbishop Vladimir of Dmitrov, head of the Theological Academy there, told Western journalists that three-quarters of those who applied to the theological seminaries had to be turned down for lack of space.

There are three seminaries, at Zagorsk, Leningrad and Odessa. Two theological academies, at Leningrad and Zagorsk, provide for post-graduate study. The seminary course alone lasts five years, and a further four may be spent at the academy. The higher course is also taken by priests during their active service. Between them the seminaries can train some 700 students at any one time: about 300 at Leningrad, 300 at Zagorsk, and between 100 and 150 at Odessa.

The atheist press would claim that many of those who apply to train for the priesthood do so through misplaced ambition, greed or laziness. Those who, they admit, are sincere, they claim are so merely through ignorance and narrow-mindedness. There may indeed be truth in some of their allegations in a minority of cases. The temptation of ambition may be strong, since those who choose to climb the ladder of the church hierarchy can reach positions of some influence. High church officials have, for instance, been used by the government as unofficial ambassadors abroad.

Nevertheless, even the atheist press sometimes admits that the majority of seminarians are sincere in their vocation. *Kazakhstan Truth* (5 March 1966) reports a young man who has been 'converted' to atheism after his theological training as saying that he and his classmates were 'all sincerely dedicated to God'. An unusually sensitive Soviet atheist booklet on the present situation of believers, entitled *In the Age of Temptation*, by Yu. Pishchik, publishes on p. 94 an interview with a young ex-priest. He makes a distinction between the attitude of the seminarians and those in the academy. It would appear that those who wanted an easy life chose an academic rather than a pastoral career:

□

'When I left school, my father entered me for the theological seminary. There everything seemed clear and easy to understand. I read a lot of books—I have always loved reading. However it is only now that I realise that I read many things without thinking about them, just absorbing.

'I particularly loved the *Lives of the Saints*. The example of the Saints in their courage and fortitude and their dedication to their ideal appealed to me. We lived frugally— there was no excess in those post-war years—and I thought that I too must make the sacrifices that the Saints had made.

'I graduated from the seminary successfully and was recommended for the Academy. Life was quite different there. Most of the "academics" were not prepared to deny themselves anything . . .

'Apart from three or four none of us seriously believed in God. We knew about Him, we understood that some people did believe and they must be helped in their faith, but we could not believe in Him the way the "Holy Scripture" taught.'

☐

It is difficult to assess how close to the truth this negative picture of the Academy may be. One cannot expect one who later apostasised completely to show his past in a positive light. Nevertheless he highlights the qualities of those young men who left the seminary to become parish clergy—those who now are taking the lead in the renewal among young people.

A more sympathetic, though not uncritical, light is shed by the testimony of Vadim Shavrov, who, after being converted in a prison camp in 1954 at the age of thirty, then became a theological student at the Odessa seminary. As a convert with no church background, his impressions have the freshness of outside observation. He comments on his experiences in an autobiographical essay entitled *Spring Thoughts and Memories*[1]:

☐

[1] For more extensive extracts from the essay, see *Patriarchs and Prophets*, by Michael Bourdeaux (Macmillan, 1970), pp. 182-8.

'Of course, mixing in ecclesiastical circles I had even more opportunity than in prison camp to take stock of the Orthodox clergy. I saw among them quite a few hangers-on —greedy, unconscientious, shallow people, unworthy of their high calling. Even in the upper ranks of the clergy I met some who were weak in spirit, evasive and insincere. Fortunately though, on the whole the clergy are without doubt honest, good, Christian folk, who entered the Church with a sense of vocation. Many of them are thinking people with great experience of life.

'Seminary friends were of this type. The vast majority of them were honest, untiring workers. It is no coincidence that, among the friends who graduated with me in 1956, there occur such names as Rasnyansky, at one time quite a famous railway engineer, now known as priest-monk German; a coal-cutter, Mikhail Lukin, now a deacon; I. Silakov, formerly a philologist and art-critic, now a priest; a petty officer first class, Nikolai Zolotukhin, once a sailor in the Black Sea fleet and now a venerable priest, and many others.

'All these people, at the time of their entry into the theological seminary, were already mature; each one had made a place for himself (and not a bad one) in life. What made them exchange a respected and secure social position for that of the oft-despised priesthood? The answer is clear: they had all (with personal variations) traversed the same path as myself; *experience of life* had led them to the conclusion that only religion held the truth.'

□

This description is a far cry from the atheist's interviewee with his claims to inexperience and uncritical attitudes.

Shavrov's picture of the majority of seminary students shows them to be of impressive calibre. Even the atheist press admits this from time to time. Graduates who enter theological seminary call for adverse comment. One case is even reported of a respected atheist propagandist suddenly disappearing from his job to become a priest. A note of wondering pity is struck by Kamil Ikramov in a book called

The Talisman, in which he describes a meeting with a young country priest. We quote the anecdote in full because it also illustrates some of the problems which confront young men when they set out from seminary to minister in a backward country parish:

□

'The church at Kamenka was striking in its whiteness and its solitariness. Amongst the squat, clumsy wooden cottages built on red-brick foundations, it looked like a miracle. Even my inexpert eye could see that this church did not belong to the category of unique works of old Russian architecture, but even so it was beautiful.

'From the outside it was impossible to see whether the church was open or not. Plantains were growing between the shallow steps of the porch, and the iron gates, on which hung a massive padlock, had been painted blue. Evidently the gate and the padlock had been painted to preserve them from rust.

'I should never have found my way into the church had it not been for a middle-aged woman with incredibly piercing eyes and wearing brand-new rubber boots. After looking through the wicket-gate, when she was sure it was the church I was heading for, she came up to the porch.

' "Are you coming to us?" she asked, with a worried look. "From the district?"

' "I'm from Moscow," I replied. "I'm interested in architecture. May I look at the church?"

' "Go in, go in," she said, giving me an appraising look. Evidently she was expecting someone else.

'The tops of her boots flapping, she led me through the front garden.

'Inside the church were two more women. Both were elderly, preoccupied, tight-lipped.

' "Can you tell me whether the church was built a long time ago?" I asked them.

' "A long time ago. A long time. Under the Tsar . . . Who knows?" the one with the piercing eyes replied, looking

33

round at her companions to make sure she had not said something silly.

' "And who built it?" I asked, more for something to say than because I expected an answer.

' "Nobody knows that. Some of the old people used to know, but they're dead now ... Shistereva hasn't complained to you, has she?" she asked suddenly, as if trying to clarify our relations.

' "Now, now, Yekaterina Ivanovna," a gentle, polite male voice came from behind me. You've already been told he's from Moscow. I assure you Moscow isn't interested in your goings-on. It's someone from the district you're waiting for."

' "You don't know what a trouble-maker she is, Father." Yekaterina Ivanovna flung a malicious look at the young, dark-haired priest who was coming towards us.

'The priest smiled at me with reserve. "This is our parish council," he said, indicating the three old ladies, who became even more tight-lipped. "They're waiting for an inspection. There's a difference of opinion between the left and right sides of the choir ... But I overheard you from the sanctuary asking about the date it was built. That I can tell you. Our church was built in 1774, but the name of the architect is, unfortunately, unknown. Forgive me,"—the priest smiled again—"but I haven't been here long, only three months. I was ordained just before Easter. I haven't been able to find out more yet, but at least I know the date."

' "Amazing!" I said. "One would hardly believe that this church could have been built in the midst of the forest a quarter of a century before the birth of Pushkin ..."

'... I told the priest my thoughts. He listened to me with interest. We looked at the icons, the deep carving on their wooden cases, the winter heating system.

'The old women followed us round, watched us sullenly and kept interrupting our conversation. They had a patronising attitude towards the priest and lacked proper respect. They were put out because he had found something in common with this stranger so quickly—and with one who, moreover, was most likely an atheist.

34

' "Forgive me," I suddenly recollected myself, "but we haven't introduced ourselves . . ."

' "My name is Konstantin Vasilievich." He held out his hand and blushed for some reason . . .

' "Perhaps you'd like to look at the sanctuary?" he suggested. The proposal was made out of the blue. We all understood that he wanted to escape from the women, who are not allowed into the sanctuary.

'But there our conversation about art for some reason did not get off the ground.

' "Were you at the seminary at Zagorsk?" I asked.

' "And the Academy."

' "You're very young for that," I said.

' "What? I'm twenty-seven."

'Somewhere out of sight behind the candle-chest the members of the parish council had renewed their discussion of the machinations of the mysterious intriguer Shistereva, who had complained to someone.

' "Don't you find it depressing here?" I asked with feeling.

'Konstantin Vasilievich walked over to a high barred window, sighed, was silent a minute and then answered, without turning round:

' "The service of God is never depressing." '

□

With young men of intelligence, integrity and devotion entering its ranks, the priesthood is being renewed year by year. Unfortunately there are some who, because of their political views, are forced against their will to remain laymen. Because the Orthodox Church must in some respects accommodate itself to the State if it is to continue to exist as an official institution, those to whom the State objects for ideological reasons may find themselves refused theological training. Some of those who suffer in this way have become involved in political activities because their Christian conscience leads them to engage in a fight for social justice. Nikodim Kamenskikh was one of these. Others, like Yuri Mashkov, are merely dogged by a rebellious past.

Yuri Timofeevich Mashkov applied to the Moscow seminary in 1967 but was refused entry. Born in 1937, he had been arrested for 'teaching anarcho-communism' and given a seven-year sentence. In the prison camps he had become a Christian, and his one thought on his release was that of training for the ministry. In 1967 he was again arrested, on the Finnish border, trying to defect to the West. His story, which is told in the Russian emigré journal *Grani*, no. 85, pp. 188–92, says:

☐

'Mashkov explained that he wanted to reach the West for a single reason—in order to enter a theological faculty at a foreign university and receive a higher theological education. It appeared that he had been refused entry to the Moscow theological seminary because of political unreliability . . .'

☐

Mashkov was given a savage sentence of thirteen years' prison and three years' exile. His wife Valentina, who had been with him, received ten years. She was pregnant at the time of the escape attempt and their daughter was born during their trial.

Nikodim Kamenskikh, on the other hand, succeeded in entering Odessa theological seminary, and in 1967 was in his second year. Kamenskikh came from Kirov, where the previous year a number of churches had been forcibly closed, including Kamenskikh's own parish church. In June 1966 twelve believers from the Kirov region signed a letter to the Patriarch protesting at the closure of churches and persecution of believers in their area, and at the Patriarchate's refusal to help them resist the authorities. One of the signatories was Nikodim Kamenskikh.

Kamenskikh was also friendly with the instigator of the protest, Boris Talantov, an Orthodox layman and outspoken writer on the unlawful interference of the State in Church affairs. Talantov was in fact arrested in 1969 for his activities and died in prison two years later. In April 1967 Talantov wrote to Kamenskikh at the Odessa seminary giving him news of the aftermath of the protest. Believers in

Kirov were being harassed once more. The letter never reached Kamenskikh. It fell into the hands of the *Inspector*, the lay head of the seminary. On 26 April he invited Kamenskikh to his office:

☐

'The *Inspector* said gently to Nikodim, "I'm glad that this letter fell into my hands and nobody else's. Do you want to finish your course?"

' "Yes, I do."

' "Then just take this piece of paper and pen and write me a refutation of Talantov's *Open letter from Kirov believers*."

' "I can't do that—the *Open letter* told the truth, and I as a Christian must defend the truth."

'The *Inspector* became persuasive. "Just write me a refutation and I won't show it to anyone, no-one will know about it. Don't you remember, you told me last autumn that you had signed this letter, and I never told anyone. I won't show your refutation to anyone either, and when you leave the seminary I'll give it back to you."

' "No, I can't write the statement you want me to, because it would be a lie."

'The *Inspector* threatened, "Well, then we'll have to expel you from the seminary."

' "Do what you want, but I can't sign the statement you ask for. Give me Talantov's letter—it's addressed to me."

' "I shall not give you Talantov's letter—it's a document which proves your criminal liaison with Talantov. If you sign a statement as I have said, you will finish your course here in peace, but if you refuse to make a statement we shall expel you and you'll be in trouble."

' "Do what you want, but I refuse to make the statement you demand."

' "All right then, I'll give you time to think seriously about your future, but after Easter I'll talk to you again." '

The *Inspector* subsequently used all the pressure he could to make Kamenskikh change his mind. He tried to recruit Kamenskikh's close friends to persuade him, but to no avail. All his colleagues in fact stood behind him in the stand

37

he made. Finally Kamenskikh was summoned, via the *Inspector*, to the local KGB. He refused to go without an official notice. An official of the Council for Religious Affairs, the government body in charge of overseeing the Church, spoke to Kamenskikh on the telephone:

'The official said, "The *Inspector* has told you to go to the KGB, has he not?"

' "Yes."

' "Why did you not go?"

' "I have had no official notification."

' "Come to my office at once and I will give you a notification."

' "No!"

' "What? . . ."

'Nikodim Kamenskikh put down the receiver at this point in the conversation and went back to the seminary. He patiently awaited the outcome.'

□

The Rector of the seminary, complaining that 'it was all the fault of him and the *Inspector*', then tried to persuade Kamenskikh to resign from his course 'voluntarily'. Kamenskikh refused. On 29 May 1967 he was formally expelled, for 'incompatibility with the spirit of the Seminary'. His petition to the Patriarch protesting against the expulsion was ignored. As a final act of discrimination, the police at Nolinsk, Kamenskikh's home town, refused to register him for residence there. Being unable to find work without a residence permit, he became homeless and destitute.

Nikodim Kamenskikh is a faithful member of the Orthodox Church, and one who passionately wanted to serve it in the priesthood. However his conscience would not let him stand aside when he saw the good of the Church flouted by the State while Church officials acquiesced. In his petition to the *Inspector* of the seminary in May 1967 he wrote:

□

'In reply to your verbal question, "Why did you sign the open letter of Christian believers of the Kirov region to

Patriarch Alexi?" I say this. "As a Christian and still more as a seminarian I could not refrain from signing this letter, since it contained facts which were well known to me personally." For this reason I again asserted the genuineness of my signature and of the contents of the document. I assure you that I am not and have never been a member of any schismatic group and am not and never have been under the influence of any person. I have always been in agreement with the teaching of the Russian Orthodox Church, I have always respected and still respect its hierarchy, but I consider it my Christian duty to support the complaints and petitions of other believers to those of the hierarchy who harm the affairs of the Church by their actions and help to bring about the closure of churches.'

□

In his protestation of loyalty to the Orthodox Church, balanced by the insight that the Church is not always best served by a complete submission to the secular authorities, Kamenskikh is probably typical of a certain body of Orthodox believers, many of them young. On the one hand are the fine young men who are finding a channel for their desire to serve God in the established patterns of the priesthood. On the other are those who, like Kamenskikh, cannot keep silent about the wrongs being done to the Church, or about the injustices of the social system in the Soviet Union. The two groups are not opposed to one another. Both owe a common loyalty to the Orthodox Church and its spiritual leaders. Their activities, within and without the establishment, complement one another.

Among the circle of lay Christians with a concern for human rights and justice, leaders have arisen. Some of them have had a good deal of influence on young people. Anatoli Emmanuilovich Levitin, who served two prison sentences and was finally allowed to emigrate to the West following his release in 1973, was one of these. His home, until he came under too close supervision by the KGB, was the venue for a wide variety of thinking Muscovites, many of them young people, many of them Christians, and many of them involved in the Human Rights Movement as Levitin was himself. No-one was ever turned away because of his views, but neither was Levitin equivocal about his own faith. Andrei Dubrov, one of Levitin's friends and now in emigration in Vienna, described the tiny flat in an old house on the outskirts of Moscow like this:

☐

'What most of all struck one about his home was the presence of so many young people. The tiny rooms' rang with the unceasing hubbub of young voices.

'One day a week Anatoli Emmanuilovich was "at home". When he lived in his old flat it was on a Tuesday. Sometimes the little room would be packed with twenty people, and on holidays it might be forty . . .

'Tea would be served. Vera (a young friend of Levitin's—Ed.) would bring in the chipped glasses and pour out the steaming hot tea.

'Long before the tea arrived the room would begin to fill up with smoke (though Anatoli Emmanuilovich did not smoke himself) and long arguments would be launched. Anatoli Emmanuilovich's house was the only place in Moscow where theoretical discussions went on about every subject under the sun: on the position of the Church, the history and future of Russia, on the Democratic Movement. In nobody else's flat in Moscow was it possible to talk in this way. At General Grigorenko's one was constrained by the socialist convictions of the host and could not openly speak one's mind on Communism or Lenin. At Yakir's flat conversations were on a purely practical level. At the home of the other Church writer, who writes under the name of Andrei Bogolyubov, one would be stopped at once if in the course of discussion one toppled from the heights of existentialist philosophy to the practical problems of the fight for freedom.

'But at Anatoli Emmanuilovich's one could talk and argue about what one chose. This was thanks both to the religious and political tolerance of the host, and to his massive erudition.

40

' "A corner of old Russia" was what he liked to call his flat. In his home there was an atmosphere of freedom, of religious and political tolerance. Often atheists would come in and begin long arguments about the existence of God. Anatoli Emmanuilovich always emerged victorious from such discussions.'

☐

It is to the group which grew around Levitin, and to others like it, that the young writer quoted on p. 28 referred when he spoke of 'a new ebullient force' in the Orthodox Church. These young intellectuals, loyal to the Church but not confined within the traditional forms and structure, rely for the exchange of ideas on open discussion and the circulation of *samizdat* literature. *Samizdat* means literally 'self-published'. It refers to typescripts of works which cannot be published through censored official channels. It includes all sorts of political dissent, as well as works of literature, and a large quantity of religious writing, both theology and accounts of life in the Church today. Apart from *samizdat*, the only means of publishing for Christians—outside the very limited editions of church journals such as the *Journal of the Moscow Patriarchate* permitted by the authorities—is by passing manuscripts to publishers abroad. As well as circulating in the West, Russian editions can then be brought back into the Soviet Union.

Yevgeni Barabanov is a young Orthodox layman who was deeply involved in the work of passing manuscripts to Western publishers. In September 1973 his flat in Moscow was searched by the KGB, who confiscated quantities of theological literature published abroad. Barabanov was then questioned by the police, but later released. After the experience he wrote a statement for the press. For him being a Christian means that he must fight for freedom and dignity for the individual, which includes the right to free expression of ideas. He wrote:

☐

'Why do my actions turn me into a criminal? After all this is a question of the most elementary, the most essential thing: the freedom to read and write, freedom of thought, the right of self-expression, without which a man loses himself and his own spiritual essence. These freedoms are inseparably linked with the ability to receive and to pass on any kind of information, as long as it does not contain military secrets. It is a question of the sovereignty of human thought and word as confirmed in the Declaration of Human Rights. Our government signed this along with other UNO members. Nor does Soviet legislation forbid those actions of which they are trying to accuse me. On the contrary, the confiscation of manuscripts and persecution of authors, arbitrary vetoes on publication, hindering the printing of certain works not only here but also abroad—these are clearly illegal actions which must be stopped . . .

'I have nothing to hide. I can speak openly about my actions before my nation and before the world. Let those people take cover who fear the light of publicity and who persecute the free word. I did send manuscripts and documents to the West, and I did it completely disinterestedly. I repeat: I have nothing to do with some mythical ideological enemies into whose hands I am supposed to be playing. Up to now the West has offered the only possibility of preserving these documents, saving them from physical destruction or oblivion. In doing this I was relying not only on my right of free spiritual orientation, but also being guided by the demands of Christian duty and conscience for I am convinced that genuine spiritual values cannot be created in an atmosphere of closedness and secrecy. Therefore I considered and still consider the materials that I sent out as a serious contribution to Russian culture, Russian thought and self-awareness . . .

'The aim of my statement is not self-justification. If I am arrested I shall consider it an act of gross arbitrariness. But the question is not simply concerning me, but whether Russian culture should exist independently of whether it is permitted by the official ideology and censorship. Should manuscripts perish if the authorities will not publish them here? Should people be forgotten who have already become the victims of arbitrary cruelty? To allow this would be to allow an injury not only to Russian, but to world culture. The world would not know the whole truth about our country, all the complexity of her life, the problems of her spirit, the tragic nature of her historical experience. Our century would be deprived of some of its meaning and depth if it did not draw this experience into itself. I appeal for support to all people independently of their political and religious convictions. I want people to understand the meaning of my actions. One of the serious threats hanging over the world is the constant tendency to isolation, to false secrecy, to the cover-up of evil. There would be less violence and evil in the world if everybody knew about them.'

☐

Yevgeni Barabanov was born in 1945 into a committed Communist family. His father is the director, recently retired, of a military factory in Moscow; his mother, also a Communist, is a teacher. But from childhood Barabanov had an interest in religion. His insistence on going to church and living as a committed Christian led to conflict with his family, and at the age of seventeen he left home. Anatoli Levitin took him in and helped him in his spiritual life, encouraging him in his interest in theology and religious philosophy. At one time Barabanov almost became a priest, but finally trained as an art historian, winning respect in that field. His interests are wide, but Christianity remains the inspiration of his life. Deeply convinced that religion cannot be confined within the four walls of a church building, he finds himself somewhat lonely in his conviction. The official voice of the Church speaks only on churchly matters, leaving the running of society to the Communists. Barabanov's is an isolated voice, but one which has not yet been silenced.

On church affairs too he has made known his deeply-felt opinions. In November 1973 he wrote an essay on the world ecumenical movement, entitled *The Moral Pre-requisite of Christian Unity*. In it Barabanov deplores certain aspects of the ecumenical world which have become 'politicised', in

43

that words are spoken which are acceptable to both sides of a discussion, while leaving much left unsaid. He makes it clear that he understands the spiritual nature of true Christian unity and the necessity for seeking it:

☐

'It would seem that the primitive unity of the Christian Church, for which men strive so hard today, is something no less absolute than the unity of the world. At every liturgy in different parts of the globe Christians confess their faith in "one church". The Greek term "ecclesia" itself, in the definition of St Cyril of Jerusalem, means "the gathering of everyone together in unity". And in fact the unity of the Church is not an abstract concept, not an abstract sign, but the very substance of church life, confirming "the unity of men in Christ with God and the unity of men in Christ amongst themselves". The unity of the Church—which St Paul defines as "the body of Christ"—is essentially supernatural and represents in our divided world the beginning of that new existence which we should all realise in our own life. However, all this does not mean that unity as the dogmatic essence of the Church and its functional norm is empirically realised in world history. On the contrary, the Church is divided into denominations and local churches at enmity with one another, and Christians the world over are seeking ways to restore unity among themselves.'

☐

Barabanov does not, however, recognise in the Ecumenical movement a true expression of his own deeply felt desire for the unity of the universal Church. In an obvious reference to the silence of the World Council of Churches on many issues concerning human rights in the USSR, he accuses church leaders of 'false representation': the masking of the real situation by a formula of words which can be interpreted according to the views of the speaker. This is what Barabanov understands by 'politicisation': expediency is sacrificed for moral integrity, and the peace which is proclaimed is no peace. Before true unity can be attained, Barabanov maintains, Christians must be living out Christ's command to love our neighbour, fleeing from the repetition of high-sounding phrases about peace and justice to a practical expression of the unity of the body of Christ. He closes his essay with a challenge to the Churches:

□

'Has Christianity really lost the initiative in spiritual life too? In its moral reactions the non-religious world of today more often than not outstrips the Church. It is these people who, via their "non-religious" committees and leagues, talk about suffering and help those deprived of rights. It was not the World Council of Churches but Amnesty International which actually responded to the appeals of the Baptist prisoners ... The Churches are meanwhile preoccupied with the search for their unity. Their representatives meet together as before, read reports to one another, make diplomatic trips and pilgrimages. They live as before in an artificial world of general theoretical problems and dogmatic arguments. They seriously hope that when these arguments finish, the long-awaited Christian unity will come. But if such diplomatic unity does come one day, it will be just as futile a political fiction as, say, that "friendship of nations", whose governments were reconciled only yesterday and concluded profitable trade agreements.

'But this is not the kind of unity that Christians need. Having forefeited their moral sensitivity to testimonies of evil and suffering, do they really remain with Christ and constitute His body? And is the moral foundation of the Gospels in this case not that primary initial prerequisite, without which true Christian unity is impossible?'

□

In September 1973 Mikhail Agursky, a well-known figure in the Soviet human rights movement, appealed to Western Christians to defend Yevgeni Barabanov, who was in immediate danger of arrest. Later, Yevgeni Kushev, a young Orthodox poet who left the Soviet Union at the beginning of 1974, said: 'The atmosphere surrounding Yevgeni Barabanov is now such that he may be arrested ... They have turned his parents against him. If he is forgotten in the

45

West, then he will certainly be arrested.' An urgent telephone call from Barabanov in September 1975 warned his friends in the West that he was now threatened with compulsory detention in a psychiatric hospital. This form of repression of dissenters is increasingly being used by the Soviet government. The first step is frequently for the threatened man to be called for a medical examination by the local military commission as if he was about to be called up for military service. This Barabanov has already undergone. If voluble protests in the West do not deter the authorities, this sanest of men may be shut in with the mentally ill and possibly treated with drugs which affect the personality.

Let there be no mistake: Yevgeni Barabanov is not typical of Russian Orthodoxy today, or even of its younger generation. He is disturbed by those in the Church whose Christianity is kept in a separate compartment from their everyday existence no less than by those who let their politics influence their religion. In striving to bring his beliefs to bear on all aspects of life, he meets with opposition from the hierarchy and incomprehension from the laity.

Nevertheless the Soviet government's hope that the Orthodox Church will become an anachronism and die a natural and unmourned death has yet to be fulfilled. Young people in the Church's ranks ensure that it will have a future. Some, submitting themselves to the established order, dedicated themselves to serve in the priesthood. Others feel strongly that changes will have to be made if the Orthodox Church is to have a significant impact on a secular, atheist-educated society. Still there is nothing which could be called a mass movement of young people to the Orthodox Church. The new intellectual movement is confined to the major cities and university towns: in the provinces young people are less ready to risk jobs and status through association with the Church. The element of quantity is not yet present; but quality there most certainly is.

ORIGINAL THOUGHT and creative writing are one of the marks of a renewal in the Church, especially when it touches educated people. In the Orthodox Church, some young people have made their presence felt by expressing their thoughts on the position of the Church today. Such works cannot of course be published through official channels, but circulate privately amongst those who wish to read them. Mikhail Meerson-Aksyonov, a close friend and disciple of Anatoli Levitin, is now in the West, but his essay *The People of God and the Pastors* was written while he was still in the Soviet Union. It was first published abroad by the *Messenger of the Russian Student Christian Movement* (no. 104/105, 1972, pp. 101–26).

The People of God and the Pastors is a reflection on the history of the Russian Orthodox Church and on how this has shaped the Church's present form. In particular Aksyonov is concerned with the relationship between laity and clergy, a subject which interests many parts of the Church today. Clearly, he regards aspects of the Church's traditional forms as inappropriate to present-day society. A Church which for hundreds of years was part of the structure of an imperial state now finds itself, like the primitive Church, a minority in a secular society. Adaptation is difficult, but Aksyonov points the way back to a more New Testament-based understanding of the nature of the Church and its relation to 'the world'. He believes that the emphasis must shift away from a Church heavily dominated by its priestly caste to one in which the lay member plays an active part. Without this, he implies, the Orthodox Church will never have a really widespread appeal to ordinary Soviet people. The responsibility for this change he lays squarely on the shoulders of the ordinary believer. Not for him to sit back and criticise the hierarchy—he himself must learn to play a fuller part in the witness and renewal of the whole community. Aksyonov at no time shows himself anything but a true and loyal son of the Church, but one with a great deal to offer it in the way of creative thought and vision for the future.

In the following pages are two extracts from *The People of God and the Pastors*. In the first, Aksyonov looks at the history of the Church before the Revolution. In the second, he examines its position today. Some historical background will be needed in order to understand his argument.

Orthodoxy first came to Russia in the ninth century. In 988 it was made the official religion of the princedom of Kiev, the earliest Russian civilisation, by Prince Vladimir, later canonised by the Russian Church. When, in 1237, the invading Mongols destroyed Kiev, the Church survived and flourished. The Mongol pagans who later were converted to Islam did not try to impose their religion on the vassal states of Western Russia, which they dominated for several centuries. During this time of national tragedy came a great flowering of Russian Christianity. Rural areas were Christianised as never before. The monastic movement was born and flourished, as young men gathered round great teachers and sought to concentrate their lives on spiritual things by seeking a simpler way of life. St Sergius of Radonezh founded the great monastery at Zagorsk which is still the centre of the Russian Orthodox Church. His saintly life was an inspiration to many. Ever since this era of enthusiasm monasticism has been a powerful force in the Church. The clergy are still divided into two categories: the 'black' clergy, or monks, who are celibate, and from whom bishops and the rest of the hierarchy is chosen; and the 'white' clergy, the parish priests, who have to marry and are thus excluded from higher office.

During the thirteenth and fourteenth centuries the Church was a rallying-point for Russian nationalism, giving them a sense of identity in their subjection to the Mongol infidels. It was also a time when culture and the arts were almost entirely inspired by religious themes. The greatest icon-painters of the century, Theophan the Greek and Andrei Rublev, were the pinnacle of this form of art and have never been equalled. During a period of political uncertainty, the Orthodox Church had become a truly national institution.

The Mongol power crumbled in the fourteenth century, and a new Russian state emerged, dominated this time by Muscovy. Following an attempt by the Eastern Church to make peace with Rome in 1444, the Russian Orthodox Church broke away from Constantinople and for the first time appointed its own Patriarch. More and more the Church was becoming identified with the nation. By the seventeenth century Patriarch Nikon was declaring that the Tsar and the Patriarch were joint heads of both church and state.

This close identification of the secular with the sacred authority was to have evil consequences for the Church. Peter the Great, who became Tsar in 1696, was not prepared to share his power. The Church remained firmly established as the national religion, but was subordinated to the secular authorities. Peter set up a government department to administer church affairs. The Overprocurator of the Holy Synod, a government appointee, had virtually complete control of the Orthodox Church.

At the same time, the Church lost its moral influence on government, which up to that time had been strong. Society became increasingly secularised. Peter's westernisation of the country extended to the importation of Western European culture, including the philosophy of the French Enlightenment with its rejection of Christianity. The educated sector of society from this time on largely deserted the Church.

For almost the whole of the eighteenth and nineteenth

centuries the Orthodox Church remained a national institution with very little true religious life. The Tsars regarded it as useful in reinforcing the authority of government, while at the same time disregarding its teachings. The lower echelons of society were expected to give their complete allegiance to Orthodoxy, and those who did not were persecuted. In spite of this, various sects, both Western Protestants and indigenous Russian movements, grew and flourished. With both the intelligentsia and many of the lower classes leaving its ranks, Orthodoxy was at a low ebb.

Spiritual life, however, did survive. For example, in the nineteenth century a number of 'elders'—monks of acknowledged wisdom and experience—created spiritual centres of the monasteries in which they lived, and to which multitudes flocked to learn from them. Among them was Father Amvrosy of Optina Pustyn, who was the model for Father Zossima in Dostoevsky's novel *The Brothers Karamazov*. Towards the end of the nineteenth century an awakening began which demanded a greater freedom for self-determination in the Church, not least within the local congregations. The Patriarchate had been abolished by Peter the Great, and Orthodox believers wanted to see the office restored. It was not until after the Revolution, in 1917, that Patriarch Tikhon was elected, the first Patriarch for 200 years. In the context of this development, Aksyonov's thoughts are not a purely post-revolutionary phenomenon: he belongs to a force within the Church which dates back before the beginning of the twentieth century.

□

THE PEOPLE OF GOD AND THE PASTORS by *Mikhail Meerson-Aksyonov*

The foundation of the Priesthood

The hierarchy instituted by the Saviour Himself in the persons of the Apostles formed the core of the emergent Church, and from the very beginning was marked by two fundamental characteristics given by its divine Founder. First, just as Jesus was sent by His Heavenly Father into the world, He in His turn sends His Apostles into the world (the Greek *apostolos* means messenger) see John 17, v. 18. Second, as He Himself, 'the Son of Man came not to be served but to serve' (Mark 10, v. 45), so the disciples too are sent into the world to serve (Matthew 10). To serve the Saviour is not only to preach the Kingdom of Heaven, but also to enter in part into His power. Not only did the hostile spirits of evil, uncleanness, sickness and death flee before His face, but even the tangible material world—as for example in the miracle of the feeding of the hungry crowds on five loaves—became malleable to His divine touch.

From the very beginning the institution of deacons, mentioned in the sixth chapter of the Acts of the Apostles, bears witness to the fact that the young Church immediately followed the Lord's example in its readiness to serve the world in its unavoidable material needs. This dual purpose in the hierarchical functions of the Apostles, called to service and prayer and the Word, and of the deacons (*diakonos* = servant), appointed to 'serve tables', became the basis of the wholeness and the boundaries of the Christian community (Acts 6, vv. 2–5).

But the Church's life was not limited to these two forms of service. According to the teaching of St Paul the Church is the Body of Christ, in which each Christian is an essential member, fulfilling His unique personal function (I Corinthians 12). All service in the Church is God-inspired, for 'all have drunk of the same Spirit' (I Corinthians 12, v. 13), and therefore there can be no uninspired work within the Church, however insignificant it may appear from the outside. And all forms of service in the Church are equally worthy, since each one is imbued with the whole nature of the Body, which is the prime source of its life and activity. This teaching of the Apostle Paul about the Church and the structure of the primitive Christian Churches are striking in their harmony, in which it would be impossible to imagine any opposition between the faithful and the hierarchy. The bishop depends on all the other Christians just as they do on him; he stands before them in the administration of the sacraments, but the service is the prayers of all the 'royal priesthood, the holy people' (I Peter 2, v. 9).

When did it happen, then, this destruction of the organic unity of the Church? When did the community become divided into clergy and laity, which grew more and more isolated from one another until finally the Old Testament division into the faithful and the unapproachable, closed Levitical priesthood reappeared? Just as long as the Church, as a God-inspired, corporate organisation, existed in secular society with its alien nature without becoming mixed with it, it kept its wholeness and its proper boundaries so as not to lose its ability to interact positively with the unbelieving world. But when the Imperial power, calling itself Christian, took upon itself the missionary function of the Church, and the Church was forced to take on many secular obligations, when her God-given nature was arbitrarily fused with the pagan structure of the Empire, the proper boundaries of the Church were destroyed.

While the existence of Christians in the form of small communities scattered amongst a heathen world demanded the maximum of active devotion from each believer, in the conditions of an Orthodox state, which automatically turned everyone into a Christian, this active participation began to diminish. Religion, ceasing to be a cause for rejoicing, gradually became commonplace. But this does not mean that the Spirit evaporated from the earth and all religion became shallow—it simply had to seek new forms. In an ideologically uniform society there developed a spiritual polarisation which led to the birth of monasticism. In conditions of unity of belief, the criterion adopted for distinguishing true religion was that of intensity of the spiritual life. Those who wanted to consecrate their lives to Christ had to separate themselves from the Christian society and become monks— different from the rest. (Russian *inok* = monk, from *inoi* meaning different—Ed.) If previously those who turned from the world to Christ had to abandon their individual un-

52

belief and enter the community of the faithful, now the seeker for God had to leave the society of lukewarm believers and strive for individualistic expressions of faith. The socially oriented ideal of early Christian spirituality, the conscious *salvation in collective* terms, was replaced by the ideal of *individual* salvation.

If previously salvation had been the gift of God, coming to each community of believers in the Eucharistic act, now salvation had to be obtained by ascetic observances, by which the Holy Spirit could be won. Many of the good deeds inseparable from the Gospel, which had been an essential part of the interaction between the Christian and the world, lost their straightforward meaning to take on a spiritualised interpretation. Divorced from the *condition humaine*, spirituality was refined into the making of subtle distinctions in the spiritual sphere, thus losing the spirit of what might be called the 'humanism of the Gospel'.

But the spiritual polarisation of the Christian community had another consequence. Monks naturally became the backbone of the Church and from their ranks the hierarchy began to be formed. Ordinary church members, continuing to live in society and occupied with the affairs of the world (culture, trade, war and daily toil), and constantly losing those most active in the Church, who became monks, were turned into spiritual parasites on the body of the hierarchy. The people of God—the active Christians of the first centuries—became sheep, losing their personal religious initiative, surrendering their will to the hands of the professional pastors and receiving the denigrating title of 'laity'. The monk thus became the spiritual mentor of the layman.

All this came about in a very natural way, without arousing disapproval or opposition from either side. The monk, taking on his own shoulders all the responsibilities of the Church, received unlimited rights to direct it as he willed.

The Church and the world — a false demarcation

Nevertheless these developments brought with them well-defined negative consequences. In the context of a non-social monastic spirituality, which developed not the breadth of faith but the depths of the spirit, the Biblical ethical norms, intended to regulate the life of the believer in society, lost their literal force, and took on a purely spiritual connotation. According to monastic teaching, the life of the laity, which contained elements which resisted the application of this sort of ethics, was only superficially covered by the otherworldly interpretation of the faith.

This does not mean that the demands of religion became any less; on the contrary, in the monastic system they became more rigorous, but at the same time developed a nihilistic attitude to the world. This is understandable. Creativity in religion became the domain of the monasteries, for whom 'the world' (which included the Christian community), became the antithesis of the monastery, identified with the breeding-ground of sin. Salvation from sin meant a retreat from the world into the wilderness or behind the walls of the monastery.

Life in society, then, the cause of the 'leakage' of spirituality both in the eyes of the monks who had shunned it and of the laity whose religious ideal now became the monastery, held no spiritual value. According to this scale of values, which was henceforth imposed upon the whole Christian community, the highest point was the hermit, the man of prayer, and the lowest was the layman. The entire varied sphere of human activity, inasmuch as it was not directly related to the Church, was excluded from this scale. Human life itself, with its essential elements of labour, the family, and culture, was held to have no religious significance; and since the Christian community was uniform, any system of values which contradicted this was outlawed and completely lost its hold. The Church tolerated 'the world', and since everyone cannot become a hermit, even taught condescendingly that 'salvation is possible in the world', but with open reference to human weakness.

Thus the person who aspires to the 'angelic band' but is unable to renounce his own humanity is caught in an insoluble dilemma. His inner, spiritual life strives towards

54

superhuman virtues, while his exterior, social life, deprived of religious and moral guidance, is plunged into the chaos of lawlessness.

Thousands, tens of thousands, of saints succeeded in overcoming this dualism, in giving active expression to their spiritual power, and became Christ's lights in the world. But millions and tens of millions of ordinary monks and lay people failed to overcome it. The personal, spiritual life became divorced from the material and social one, the spirit was detached from the body and the bond of God–manhood grew weak. For the majority, salvation became a matter of heavenly, not earthly life. The whole of man's life on earth, the interval between the christening and the funeral, had no intrinsic meaning but was to be subjected to the sole thought that death was on its way. Salvation occurred at the moment of departure, when the soul was able to leave this sinful world, and leave the prison of the body to be with God. This did not mean that every human thought was directed towards heaven—they remained very earthly—but Christian spirituality at that time did not attempt to illuminate that 'worldly' part of the soul or to bring into force in earthly life the law of *righteousness*. So the merchant traded and cheated, the warrior fought and plundered, the prince upheld justice and oppressed his people, but as the end of life approached all three took the monastic habit and left the world in order to save their souls.

The spirit of gnosticism had crept into the Biblical understanding of the incarnation. The wholly literal meaning of the Christian prayers: 'Lord Jesus, come quickly!' and 'Thy will be done, Thy Kingdom come on earth as it is in heaven' had become too spiritualised. It is easier to renounce this world for God than to ask Him to enter it, or to recognise His eternal presence in the world.

A hardening of Church structures

The dualism of this Christian consciousness is likewise reflected in Church practice. The spiritual polarisation of the community led to a situation where the full operation of the

55

charismatic gifts, once spread throughout the community, was now limited to the hierarchy, to the monastic communities and the clergy. The Church, from being an *ecclesia* —'the gathering of the people'—became the temple, confined to the house of prayer. Likewise the *litourgia*, instead of being 'communal worship', as its Greek title implies, became a ceremonial mystery performed by clerical professionals who in their turn became 'servants of the cult'.

Worship took on increasingly complex ceremonial forms and finally hardened, receiving the name of 'ritual'. By the Middle Ages creative worship had been replaced by a ritual which carried the stamp of Early Byzantium and its culture, which made its way through history to the Russian Church and has come down to this day having lost a great deal of its original meaning.

For the believers, the one-time active people of God, worshipping alongside the hierarchy, worship itself became entwined with the unchanging, dogmatised ritual. As in Old Testament times the presence of God was, as it were, limited to the confines of the Temple. The layman became the one for whom the services were performed, who would go to the pastor so that he, like a Christian high priest, might perform for money the ritual he wanted, and thus 'offer up prayers' on his behalf. All this can take on such a mechanical character that the personal link between the clergy and the believer may become irrelevant and fortuitous, like the relationship between the buyer and seller in a shop.

The community which had been the focal point of the lives of the faithful, had become the parish church, a place where Christians might come to say a prayer on their own and then go away! While at one time the bishops and clergy had been wedded to the community in a union which only death could dissolve, now the bishop was not bound irrevocably to his diocese nor the priest to his parish; a bishop could be a bishop without a flock, having never set eyes on his sheep, and a priest might move endlessly from one parish to another.

But this could not have happened were it not for the growing mutual isolation of the clergy and the laity, who became two disconnected layers, each existing in a completely separate dimension with its peculiar psychology and world-view. The internal canonical and liturgical structure of the Church, formulated in Byzantium in the fifth to eighth centuries, contributed to this process of isolation. Formed in the age of monasticism, the structure was overlaid with a deep layer of Monophysite asceticism (a heresy which denied the humanity of Christ and thence condemned the physical as evil—Ed.).

The unnatural existence of the Church in the Orthodox empire led to a spiritualisation of its consciousness, to a turning away from real life, and to a merely symbolic likeness to the early Christian Church of the Apostles. While in the primitive Church everything had an immediacy drawn from its living incarnational reality, in the Byzantine Church everything became a symbol. The Apostle's staff, essential for long and exhausting missionary journeys, became the episcopal crozier, merely a burden which the bishop had to have a special chaplain to bear. The chief weapon of the Christian in the world is the spiritual sword of the Word of God, which has become symbolised only in the epigonation and the mace taken by the priest before the service. All the priestly vestments, all his gestures, are no more than a symbol and a representation. The gold, the purple, pearl and brocade symbolise the heavenly power and earthly humiliation, the suffering, bonds and toil.

The intensely active existence of the primitive Church, thanks to whom the world became Christian, is merely symbolised in ecclesiastical life, is merely called to mind in the words of the lectionary. Who would recognise in the modern deacon, whose incomprehensible words echo down the Church, the co-worker of the Apostles, called by God to be a servant of men, embodying the social function of the Church?

There came a time when the real life of the Church was transformed into representation and symbol, whose very meaning has been forgotten and lost.

□

The second extract, which follows, deals in its first part with the 'Living Church' movement which existed in the Orthodox Church between 1922 and 1927. Its supporters have since been christened the *obnovlentsy*, meaning renovators or renewers, which is translated here as 'reformers'. People joined the movement for many reasons, some seeing a genuine hope for the bringing of Orthodoxy into the twentieth century. But they were exploited by the Communists in an attempt by the regime to bring the Church under its domination. Aksyonov examines it from the point of view of those who wanted to accommodate the Church to a new form of society.

At the *Sobor* (Council) held in 1917, the Orthodox Church elected as its head Patriarch Tikhon, and for a few years enjoyed comparative peace and freedom. In 1922 the Patriarch was arrested following the State's attempt to confiscate Church property, including liturgical vessels. With the Church for the time being bereft of its leader, the 'Living Church' attempted to win influence. In August 1922 the Council of the Living Church passed the following resolution:

'The Council affirms that every honourable Christian should take his place among these warriors for humanitarian truth and use all means to realise in life the grand principles of the October Revolution.'

Clerics were forced to support this resolution and take an oath of loyalty to the government. Those who refused could be shot, as was Metropolitan Veniamin of Petrograd after a trial on 12 August 1922. Not surprisingly, however, the movement failed to gain the support of the majority of believers, who remained loyal to their imprisoned Patriarch. When he was released, in June 1923, it was on condition that he declared his own loyalty to the revolutionary government. In humiliating himself in this way he effectively cut the ground from under the feet of the 'Living Church', by removing the conflict between Church and State loyalties.

The Orthodox Church avoided deeper schism, and although the 'Living Church' existed formally for another four years, it completely lost its influence.

☐

Adaptation and controversy — Orthodoxy and the Soviet State

The Revolution took the Church unawares for two reasons. Firstly, Orthodoxy had developed both historically and psychologically under an absolutist regime, and had never conceived of existence without it. Secondly, its protracted but short-sighted opposition to the growth of secularisation, its hostility to the new and active social forces and its compromising alliance with the autocracy with its immovable conservatism all made its reorientation to the new situation more difficult. The State protection which had solved so many of the Church's external problems for it disappeared. The historically established form of State religion perished. As one ecclesiastical paper put it at the time, the decree on the separation of Church and State separated the soul from the body. And this spells death. Anti-religious legislation and practice set out systematically to dismember the Church.

The enthusiasm with which the State entered into the battle against the Church and the success of atheism, however, would be incomprehensible without the realisation that victorious secularisation, henceforth the State ideology, had its sources in religion. Secular society bypassed the Church and made its ideals those very things which had been lost to historical Orthodoxy.

While Orthodox spirituality was characterised by the spiritualisation of the ethical side of Christianity, and its Church practice by an escape from social involvement, the keystone of the new ideology became that side of Biblical teaching which had been lost to Orthodoxy—social ethics. It is no accident that the slogans of the new order were taken from Scripture itself: 'If any man will not work, let him not

59

eat' (II Thessalonians 3, v. 10); 'And they shall beat their swords into ploughshares, and their spears into pruning-hooks' (Isaiah 2, v. 4); 'Come now, you rich, weep and howl for the miseries that are coming upon you . . . you have laid up treasure for the last days . . . behold the wages of the labourers who mowed your fields, which you kept back by fraud, cry out . . .' (James 5, vv. 1–4); 'So the last will be first, and the first last' (Matthew 20, v. 16).

To the spirit of religious individualism and withdrawal from society was opposed that of collectivism; to the abstract—striving towards liberation from the body, towards the 'angelic band', and to spirituality—materialism, the physical, to the point of rejection of the very concept of the spirit; to the exclusive concentration on the next world—the building of an earthly city and a human society without conflicts; to faith, in which reason had no part to play—reason which would destroy faith.

In the opposition of these two ideologies it seems that the separation over the years of the two original religious functions of the Church are placed in symbolic contrast to one another: prayer to God and the service of men in society. The State had, as it were, symbolised the role of the servant, taking on itself the diaconal function of 'serving tables', placing it in opposition to the religious enthusiasm of the Apostolic mission of 'prayer and the Word'.

When the Church forgot in part about its existence as a 'gathering of the people' (*ecclesia*) and its calling to 'communal worship' (*litourgia*), the State took upon itself the Church's work of salvation, tinting the unification of its people and its social responsibilities with a sacramental hue.

The strength of contemporary secularisation lies in that, in its view, the seven New Testament deacons have been opposed to the apostles, and both sides have forgotten that God's blessing rests on both kinds of servants, who are rooted in the very nature of the Church.

Two paths were open to the Church in the new situation: to adapt, and in its adaptation to do all that was asked of it; or to maintain complete independence and make no concession whatever to the demands of the age. The first path promised some sort of future, but the second heralded the approach of Doomsday. At the parting of the ways the Church was unable to take the strain—the two tendencies were too strong in her—and underwent schism. The Patriarch and his followers took the path of independence, wishing to preserve untouched the historical form of Orthodoxy.

But a part of the Church was attracted by the other, 'new' path. The positive side of the secularisation which had triumphed throughout the country, the 'reformers' decided, could be used. They realised that if the Church wanted to retain its role of mother and mentor of the *whole* people, it must formulate answers to the problems of life in society and, abandoning its traditional sluggishness, plunge into dynamic action in society. In the interests of the renewal of the Church the 'reformers' decided to 'use' the revolutionary government, forgetting the historical experience of church–state unity. In its blindness the 'renewal' fell for the old temptation of Orthodoxy, which once more was to cost the Church very dear. The 'reformers' transformed the traditional established Orthodoxy into an alliance of a social Christianity with a socialist government, staking its survival on government support against the 'Old Church'—that is to say the Orthodox Church.

The 'reform' came to grief because it had not taken account of two factors: firstly that the strength of Christianity lies not in the support of the rulers of this age, nor in the ability to adapt quickly and without regard for principle to the changing backcloth of society, but in the spirit and nobility of its moral position; and secondly, that the new order was as a matter of principle hostile to all religion, and the more so to 'rose-tinted' religion which claimed to be an equal co-worker with the State, and therefore in spiritual competition with it. The 'reformers' missed the major point: the ideological-spiritual nature of secularisation as a *faith* which sought to replace Christianity.

The 'reform' did contain a very valuable beginning, which

in theory could have transformed the Church from a relic of a dying age into an organisation embracing the whole nation. But in the eyes of the members of the Church it compromised itself by its unprincipled antagonism to the Patriarchal Church so that even its good attempts at reform were suspected as being secretly aimed at undermining Orthodoxy. The State, of course, had not the slightest interest in the reform of the Church and even less concern that the 'reformers' should carry out their reforms with the support of state power.

For these reasons, when the temporary head of the Patriarchal Church, Metropolitan Sergii, agreed to all the demands of the State, which had been an obstacle to his predecessors, the 'reform' lost the support of the government. The Metropolitan announced his open support of the authorities as the national government, recognising their right of control over the Church administration. Now membership of the hierarchy was limited to those who supported the principle of co-operation with the government. Metropolitan Sergii demanded that all those members of the clergy who did not sympathise with the new course should resign. Those bishops who refused to be associated with it were defrocked . . .

The Church in today's world

The Church was indeed founded to be an island of freedom. But what power can give it external freedom apart from its own internal freedom, the freedom of the Spirit which indwells the Church? Internal freedom can be measured by the presence of creativity. The creative spirit is above all a free spirit which abhors routine. In a sense freedom is the same as life, because life is constantly creating new forms. Death is made up of two processes: ossification and decay.

The early Christian Church was the home of genuine creative freedom. The ancient world around it decayed, collapsed and died, but Christianity created a new world in the place of the old. Indeed, the growth of this new life in the power of the Spirit in its turn created the best conditions for the enthusiasm which made Christians stand out in the eyes of ordinary people. For the Christian the world was seen to be continually being transformed and renewed, and this creative view of the world was reflected in the creation of prayers, new forms of worship, Christian art, icons which were the living, developing expression of continual thanksgiving. And in this Church was the image of the Israel of God, whose creative religious life was constantly compared with the words of Holy Scripture, and, when it did not live up to them, strove still harder. Every one of the Psalms is a part of one eternal song, and the prayers of the Church later took up this improvisation of the repenting, dying, saved and thankful religious spirit.

The pagan who came into the Church would immediately find himself in an atmosphere of the unceasing creativity of God in man, and in the light of this creativity the activity of the world would seem to him so wretched that it would lose its former devotee for ever. For the first few centuries the fire of creativity in the Church burned so strongly that the attention of the whole population was attracted. Even the theological arguments, which to us seem so abstract and comprehensible only to the specialist, occupied the thoughts of ordinary people, in the same way that international football or chess matches do today. One of the holy fathers says that even in the market, buyer and seller would argue about the nature of the unity of the Father and the Son after their deal was concluded. The whole people was in the Church, and so naturally they brought into it the noise of the marketplace. Complete silence is only found in a cemetery. The Church was still unafraid of the bustle and noise of the crowd, did not hasten to encase itself in a gilded shrine or to separate itself from the world by an invisible barrier of spiritual pride.

But when, after several centuries, this separation of the people of God into clergy and laity came about, and religion became the professional affair of the former and the salutary obligation of the latter, human noisiness left the Church, and solemnity reigned. One generation after another was to enter the temple and become accustomed to the ceremonial carried on as it were without their participation and on their behalf; to repeat in an unknown language, or at best an archaic one, words of supplication; to fill the freshness and life of their souls with petrified ritual forms.

Wherever the life of the Church is limited to the form of worship alone, the divine gifts, of their own nature dynamic, become buried talents. The action of the human will ceases to respond to the promptings of the Spirit, loses its place in the Church and abandons it. The living organism of religion becomes a ritual.

When the people became guests in the Church, is it surprising that human creativity, divorced from faith, went the way of secularisation, and that the intelligentsia—the most creative section of society—left the Church?

In our time human creativity, bereft of the Holy Spirit and having exhausted its own innate power, has begun to destroy itself and is faced with a dilemma—either return to the Church or die. Contemporary man, the son of the secular era, lost in a closed world of merely human values, necessarily questions religion on those things to which it alone holds the answers. He sees the Church as the source of his last hope. But if he goes into an Orthodox Church or one of the remaining monasteries he finds himself in a museum, a place where some incomprehensible activities are preserved as living relics, wonders of an age lost in the past. With disillusioned eyes he looks at this beautifully conserved reality which outwardly confirms everything which the unbelieving world has said . . .

The Church does not have the right today to cut itself off, to be an archaism, a museum of restored ancient monuments, into which the troubled and creative human soul may not come. The Church cannot remain a world of its own, with on the one side the hierarchy—a hereditary Levitical company with traditional, unchangeable presuppositions—and on the other side the dumb 'flock' of the laity. It must find a place for the modern man with his active, dynamic, cosmic consciousness, his social and cultural interests and creative potential.

But can the Russian Orthodox Church of today, heir of the conservative caste-consciousness of the clergy and the lack of initiative of an institution dependent on the government, rise to the demands of the contemporary world? If the Church is to be determined by its past and present, then it cannot do it; but Christianity is a living force in history and will not become petrified. The one and a half thousand years of the Christian empire is at an end, and it is time the Christian community everywhere hastened to strip off its ecclesiastical trappings. Today the Christian does not live in the midst of fellow-believers, but amongst people who have their own ideas which may even be hostile to religion, who regard it with scepticism, apprehension, or merely with curiosity. Today the Church is called to bear conscious witness to all people of its hope, and retreat from the world is certainly not the best means of witness.

Every age has its own ways of seeking God; the apostles found God in the market-place, hermits followed Him into the wilderness. On every side the myriad voices of the world are showing us where in our day His presence is being sought, where we must bear the light of faith which He has lit in us.

While during the long period when the Christian community was divided into laymen and monks it was possible to be content with an individual path of salvation, now the world around us with all its groanings reminds us that we cannot be saved alone. When both in ourselves and in those around us the virtues of which the Gospels teach are so rare, it is not the time to hedge them round with a spiritualised meaning. When there is so much material prosperity in the world it is premature to think about the life beyond the grave. In an age when humanity is taking a back seat it is time to think about the Christian sources of humanism.

The shortage of monasteries must not be attributed only to ill-will, but seen as a sign of the times. It is not the monks who must now be the vanguard of the Church, nor the clergy the main instrument by which it is to work in the world. The layman himself must cease to be a mere member of the flock for which there are not enough pastors. When loneliness fills people's souls, the Christian must remember that the Lord is present where many are gathered in His name.

Our time, which has forced the Church out of its former comfortable situation, is also forcing it to concentrate all its spiritual energy, all its dynamism, to use all its faculties; and for this it is essential that it should return to the state of organic unity of all the faithful which it had in the first few hundred years of its existence. Then all Christians were 'living stones, built into a spiritual house' (I Peter 2, v. 5), all participated in the mysteries, and were not merely present at their accomplishment; all were a 'holy priesthood' and served the Church according to the gifts given them by the Spirit.

The task of the layman

It was in the most impotent century of the Russian Church— the nineteenth century—that teaching on communality was formulated. While academic theology was shot through with the spirit of clericalism, independent theology, relying on the traditions of the ancient Church and an understanding of Orthodox practice, conceived the idea of communality, according to which the whole membership of the Church along with the hierarchy made up the Body of Christ, in the whole of which the Holy Spirit dwelt in His fulness. It is characteristic that all innovations in theology came from the laity. These are the creators of the renewal of religious thought, freely expressing the experience of Christian faith: Chaadaev, Khomyakov, Solovyov, the brothers Trubetskoy, Berdyaev, Bulgakov.

It was no accident that these new impulses arose in the sphere of the Church's social activity. The hierarchy, rejecting on the one hand in the ascetic-monastic tradition any involvement in the life of society, and on the other closely bound to the State, could only be a conservative force. In addition, the system of subordination within the Church threatened any member of the clergy who dared to say an original word.

This does not mean that the episcopate was hostile to the notion of the renewal of Church life; it means only that because of its position it had lesser opportunities for creative activity. The believing intelligentsia and the parish clergy were left to take the initiative in the movement for reform. In part it was the religious and philosophical discussions which opened up a dialogue between the intelligentsia and the Church in the final years of Pobedonostsev's numbing reign, which laid the foundations of the future intensive social movement in the Church which began in 1905 and culminated in 1917 with the All-Russian General Council (which, it must be said, Russia had awaited for more than 200 years and which gave back the Patriarchate to the Church).

From the experience of Orthodoxy at the beginning of this century one may draw the conclusion that creative initiative lay with the ordinary people of the Church. It would appear that two functions characterise the Orthodox people, the indestructible mass of believers who make up the body of the Church. It preserves the Church from which the hierarchy proceeds, being of one flesh with the people. But as well as this the believing intelligentsia, a part of the laity, from Khomyakov, Dostoevsky and Solovyov to Solzhenitsyn in our day, have a prophetic function in the Church—to bear witness to the Truth. This prophetic function as it were complements the 'sacramental' function of the silent hierarchy.

However, in spite of all this, the bishops remain the 'mouthpieces' of the Church. In each period of its life the hierarchy has reflected the moods and feelings experienced by the people of the Church. It was indifferent to church reform, to politics, to social transformations, at a time when the laity too was indifferent to all these things. But as soon as the Russian intelligentsia turned to the Church, as soon as the rank and file began to talk about freedom of conscience and independence from the government, as soon as the working class became involved in the socialist movement and the war of strikes, as soon as Russian society, which had been monolithic from time immemorial, divided into several parties in the course of a single year, bishops began sending out memoranda on the transformation of the Church, each one more revolutionary than the last; the bishops and arch-bishops of the Synod rebelled against the Procurator, priests turned into socialists and organisers of Christian trade unions, and monks began to make political speeches from the platform of the Duma (the pre-revolutionary parliament —Ed.).

If today we are surprised at the indifference of the epis-copate to the life of society, the dwindling membership of the Church and the way in which Church documents bear little relation to the real state of affairs, there is no need to look further than at the mood of the parishes. Not in two or three central Moscow churches during a festival service, but some-where in the suburbs at a weekday liturgy or vespers. A quarter of the small church is filled with people, old women in headscarves, a few young women with children, oc-casionally a middle-aged man with a good-natured but flabby face. Sometimes two or three curious passers-by will drop in and stand for five minutes watching, but then, not hearing or understanding anything properly, they go away again. Not a very mighty army for the renewal of Church life.

If you were to ask any parishioner taken at random for her views on any of the subjects raised in correspondence: how she regards atheist propaganda, the Synod of Bishops of 1961, the millions of roubles donated to non-Church funds, the Patriarch's Easter message—then the meaning of a lot of high-level Church policy becomes clear. The living strength of the people has left the Church: it has gone over to pioneer building projects, to the football stadium, the cinema, the dance-hall, the pubs. And the woman is simply following the 'superstition' of her mother and her grandmother, not understanding it, and not particularly concerned about it. Why should she fight for her right to say her prayers or have her grandchildren christened without the permission of the authorities? Solzhenitsyn showed this with superb artistry in his sad tale of *The Easter Procession*.

While amongst non-Church intelligentsia, which in general knows little about the Church and does not understand her present situation very clearly, there is sharp criticism of the supreme hierarchy, in an Orthodox parish the very thought of such a thing is unheard-of. You have only to watch how people flock to services celebrated by a bishop, see how anxious they are to receive his blessing, to feel that the hierarchs are still the authoritative heirs of the Apostles, to know that the bishops are deeply bound to the people and that, to coin a phrase, the Church gets the Patriarch it deserves.

If we as Christians, not limited by holding episcopal office, with no fear of being defrocked and only risking the loss of our jobs, are afraid to confess our faith openly and only come, like Nicodemus, at night, if we regard baptism into eternal life with Christ as no more significant than collecting a passport, then how can we blame the bishops, who at least confess their faith for all to see?

Do we do much for the Church when we spend a couple of hours at the Sunday service—not counting the few pence we leave behind? Can we really say that we are active participants in that 'communal worship', that our heart is in the 'gathering of the people', that here is the whole aim of our life?

In the early days of Christianity those who confessed their faith were thrown to the lions, but the very existence of Christians was a challenge to the world. The Christians would not bow down and burn incense even to those wretched idols which the Apostle said were of no account— even at the price of their lives.

Let us take a look at ourselves and see what place the altar of the True God has amongst the range of idols to which we bow down each day. And what sort of a challenge to the world is our timid faith which hides in corners with careful submissiveness? In our heart of hearts we feel that our faith is too unworldly, that it has too few roots in this earth. Our faith, separated from works of love, seems too insipid to convince and attract the man of today who no longer believes in the abstract.

We, the anointed, instead of *witnesses* have become the little old men and women of the Church, who think the Church is a quiet haven where we may find peace after the storm-tossed sea of everyday life. There we need do no more, it is all completed, perfected, glorified, laid down long ago. Now we need only strive for our own souls to become equally perfected and glorified. Life has found its fulfilment, there is nothing more to desire and we can prepare ourselves for the grave. We confirm the judgement of outsiders that the Church is merely a survival of a past age.

Where is the restless creativity, the keenness of the searching soul, the responsibility, the purposeful activity? The Church should be the domain of the most real freedom, that very freedom which is where the Spirit of the Lord is. But where is that most creative, life-giving, and not deadening Spirit of Christ to be found amongst us?

The highest peaks of Russian theology asserted that Orthodoxy was a source of great spiritual freedom, but gave no teaching on the world, the State, or society, and left the Christian the initiative of the creative quest. He is free to choose his own position, whatever he thinks is closest to the spirit of the Gospels. But this, alas, is possible only in the realm of theology. Catholicism, which we so delight to accuse of clericalism, allows the laity today a great deal of spiritual freedom within the bounds of its dogma, telling them even in important matters not to expect ready-made answers from the clergy, but in the spirit of Christian boldness to take the responsibility on themselves; we, on the other hand, run to the priest for his blessing on the merest trifle.

The leaders of the Russian religious revival of the beginning of the century, who rejected the theological bridge between the Church and the world, were not heretics. Nearer to heresy in the Church is indifference, the legalistic horror of innovation, the pietistic inactivity arising from a fear of causing more evil, the Monophysite rejection of the world, the spiritual parasitism.

The clergy neither teach nor evangelise. But what of us, the body of the Church, who *do not bear witness, do not tell the good news?* What holds us back? If only converted Christians would cease to regard the Church as if they were casual visitors, consumers, without even the right of a 'consultative voice'. It is the intelligentsia of the Church, free from the responsibilities of the hierarchy and its innate conservatism who must prepare the way both in theory and in practice for a *new*, evangelistically-oriented Christianity in secular society.

The open discussion of ecclesiastical questions begun by A. I. Solzhenitsyn in his letter[1] may prove one of the first steps in this direction. The harm is not in the writing of such letters, harsh as they may appear, but in the fear that the *truth* about the Church—or at least some part of that truth—may damage someone or prove a temptation for some few in that, as one reply to the letter put it, 'a literary howl may inadvertently batter the whole structure of the Church'.

As if it could be patched up by silence. They have been battering it for a long time already, without our help, but not with literary words alone, but it still stands. There is a great deal of hypocrisy in this calm. Who has ever been tempted by the truth, and how many in the world have been tempted with lies? In the same way, before the Revolution, the Church opposed the giving of freedom of conscience to the people, fearing to tempt some few. As a result those 'few' left the Church altogether. But now what can one do but bury one's head in one's hands and weep? We are all afraid to let any more light into our secret corner where a thick layer of cobwebs has already shrouded the icons and the

[1] Solzhenitsyn wrote an *Open Letter* to the Patriarch at Easter 1972 criticising the silence of the hierarchy on matters of religious freedom. Subsequently it became a centre of debate amongst the Orthodox intelligentsia.

71

lamp, and we call our timidity zeal for the Church. We weep because we are crushed, we are oppressed, and so we have made ourselves comfortable in our cramped little corner. We hope to preserve the Church for God too much by human prudence.

Christians must not judge or condemn, but to them is given the opportunity for a charismatic ministry in the Church—that of *witness*. Christians are called to bear witness to their faith and hope, and indeed they must witness too about the disorders in their own house. Our age has not wearied of condemning the Church, and every schoolchild knows about its past and present sins. In our day it is thought laughable to talk about the foulness of our own nest. But we can go out and say honestly to all outside, friends and enemies: 'Yes, there are many, many things wrong in our house, but we are staying in it and invite you to come in, for it is the only house worthy of *man*, because it is the house of *God*, and we have nowhere to go apart from it—for here are the words of *eternal life*.'[1]

[1] Extracts from the essay *The People of God and the Pastors* are reproduced by permission of Norland Publishing Company, Belmont, Mass., U.S.A.

IF IN the Orthodox Church the influx of young people is a small but significant trickle, in some sections of the Baptist Church it amounts to something like a flood. Indeed the breakaway portion of the Church, which is organised outside the officially-tolerated structure, has been christened 'the young Baptists'.

Baptists are the largest Protestant group in the Soviet Union. In 1944 the All-Union Council of Evangelical Christians and Baptists was formed by an amalgamation of the two main evangelical denominations. The Union includes Mennonites, many of them of German origin and some Pentecostals; but the Lutherans, mainly in the Baltic states, and other Pentecostal communities are independent and make up the remainder of the Protestant world in the Soviet Union.

According to the atheist commentators, the majority of young people are more readily attracted to the Baptist forms of worship than the Orthodox. They find the services easier to understand, the teaching more relevant to everyday life. While it is Biblically based, most Soviet Baptist preaching deals with practical aspects of the Christian life rather than the finer points of theology. Historically a predominantly working-class movement, the Russian Baptist Church appeals to the young person in search of a simple, life-sustaining faith, whereas Orthodoxy satisfies the intellectual and the artist.

As far back as the early 1960s the appeal of the Baptist

Church to the younger generation was clearly a matter of some concern to the Soviet authorities. An attack on this influence was included in Khrushchev's great anti-religious campaign. He succeeded in pressuring the All-Union Council into accepting a set of instructions which forbade the baptism of young people under eighteen, special meetings for children and Sunday Schools. A part of the Church refused to accept such restrictions and broke away, forming their own organisation, the Council of Churches of Evangelical Christians and Baptists. Their local congregations were not permitted to register as churches, and therefore existed illegally, as they do to this day. While continually prosecuted by the authorities for its very existence, the Council of Churches—otherwise known as the Reform Baptist movement—carries on a much more open and active work amongst young people than the 'official' wing of the Church.

Not that young people are excluded from the services at registered Baptist churches. Khrushchev's instructions never forbade this. Large numbers of the young are to be seen openly taking part in worship. As in the Orthodox Church, young men are able to train for the pastorate, although the Baptist Church has no seminaries in the Soviet Union. A small number go each year to theological colleges in Western Europe, while for the rest there is a correspondence course training 200 students at a time.

Not for nothing, however, have the Reform Baptists been noted for the exceptionally high proportion of young members. On 2 May 1973, for example, the young people of the unregistered congregations in the area of Kharkov, in the Ukraine, held an Easter celebration in the open air in the country outside the city. 1,500 young people came from the churches, and some outsiders too. A report, published in the *Bulletin*, no. 12, of the Reform Baptists' Council of Prisoners' Relatives, tells of young men and girls responding to the call to commit their lives to Christ. Nevertheless the day's ending was not a happy one. Police and volunteer brigades arrived to break up the meeting. The principal preacher, evangelist Boris Zdoroviets, was arrested—only

74

a few months after his return home from a ten-year prison sentence.

The events clearly symbolise the position of the Reform Baptists vis-à-vis young people: in no area has their work been so successful, yet in no area, except perhaps that of the distribution of Christian literature, has it been more severely repressed. Again and again in the prosecutions of Christians, their work amongst young people and children has been one of the accusations brought against them. The story of the 'young Baptists' inevitably involves the story of their suffering.

About two weeks after the meeting at Kharkov, some of the same young people signed a letter of protest to Communist Party Secretary Brezhnev, complaining about further interference by the police in their affairs. This time they had been visiting friends in the village of Khudoyari, when again their gathering was disturbed by the police. After a search of the premises, Christian literature was confiscated. The words of the protest may seem naïve, but these young people are contrasting what they have been taught at school about their social system with what they experience in reality:

□

'It is strange that this should happen in our free country with its social structure which is the most advanced in the world. It is still more strange that this is not something unusual, but one of many such events which believers all over the country are reporting. Such actions by the authorities put us in much the same position as the negroes in America, and we demand freedom for Christian young people! We want, just like all young people, to be able to sing our songs freely, without the fear that our songbooks will be confiscated, we want to be able to read the Bible freely without the fear that it will be snatched from our hands, we want to be able to pray freely and visit our friends without the risk that the police will come in the middle of the night.

'Give us freedom!

'We beg you to intervene to prevent the outrageous

behaviour of the local authorities. We beg you too to order the local authorities of Shevchenko to return the literature and personal possessions which were illegally taken from us and of which we attach a list.

'The question which troubles us is this: what will happen next? This question troubles all upright people of the world, and the answer is in your hands and on your conscience.'

☐

Again, a vital aspect of the Reform Baptist movement is typified by these brave young people who are growing up to follow in their parents' footsteps. Since its beginning, the Council of Churches has not been afraid to stand up and insist on the rights which are due to the Church under the Soviet Constitution, which guarantees freedom of religion. Protest after protest has been sent to the Soviet government, to organisations such as the United Nations, and to Churches in the West.

Nevertheless, so far the authorities have turned a deaf ear. For those who are particularly active in their Churches and open in their zeal for evangelism, the state has replied with prison sentences. The Council of Prisoners' Relatives compiles careful information about all of these, and it is notable that some are very young. Aida Skripnikova was only twenty when she first incurred the authorities' displeasure by distributing handwritten leaflets on a street corner in Leningrad. When first arrested she was twenty-four, and she served a year's imprisonment. Two years later she was arrested again, this time to be sentenced to three years. A leading light in the Leningrad unregistered congregation, she had played a part in the sending of information to the West about their life.[1]

Others have been even younger at the time of their arrest. Yevgeni Rodoslavov, from Odessa, was nineteen when he was arrested in 1968 and given a savage sentence of five years in prison camp followed by five years' exile to a remote part of the Soviet Union. 180 young people from the Odessa

[1] See *Aida of Leningrad*, by Michael Bourdeaux and Xenia Howard-Johnston, Gateway Outreach, Reading, 1972.

congregation signed a protest at his sentence and the conditions of the trial. Yelena Chernetskaya and Maria Braun were arrested in 1966 for work with children in the Kemerovo region, where they ran a Sunday School with eighty members. Maria was nineteen, Yelena twenty-two. Sadly, Maria was persuaded during her sentence to abandon her faith, and now lives a very different sort of life. Yelena, so far as is known, served her five-year sentence to the end. Pyotr Bondaruk was arrested at the age of twenty-two in 1971, and sentenced to three years. His home is in Brest. Pavel Runov received an eighteen-month sentence in 1970, also at the age of twenty-two. Four others were tried along with him, including his father, pastor of the Gorky congregation. In September 1973 two young men were tried in Riga, capital of Latvia: Andrei Petrov, aged twenty-six, and Mikhail Kolesnichenko, aged twenty-nine. They were sentenced to one and three years' imprisonment, respectively, for distributing Christian literature.

In December 1970 the Council of Prisoners' Relatives held a congress which later gathered together a number of documents relating to Baptists in prison at the time. One of them was a letter from four young prisoners to young friends in their congregation. The four young women are clearly not to be discouraged by the bitter hardships of prison life. They begin their letter with a quotation from the Epistle to the Romans, chapter 8, verse 31: 'If God is for us, who can be against us?'. They go on:

□

'Dear brothers and sisters, young heirs of Christ, and the whole Church which is suffering hardship and persecution, but has remained faithful to its Lord: PEACE BE TO YOU!

'We send heartfelt greetings to you all in the name of Him who at the right time gave His life for us, who called us in our youth to follow Him, in the name of the fairest of the sons of men—*Jesus*!

'At this time we want with you to give Him the most hearty thanks and praise for both the trials and the blessings which we four prisoners—Lida, Lyusya, Nadya and Vera—

have experienced and are now experiencing during this time of separation from you.

'Praise the Lord for this temporary parting, praise Him for the trials!

'Dear friends, we know that you who are free are experiencing great troubles and oppressions . . . There is only one thing that we can say: *Our God is for us!*

'And can there be any power on earth which can force us to betray the Lord, or which can divide the people of Christ? No, no such power exists! Surely everything which touches the Church touches the apple of the Father's eye and so, dear friends, let us go forward with this in mind, united with one another and as a single family, trusting in Christ! But there is not much further to go, very little further. The day when we shall meet with our best Friend is near, when we shall be with Him in His beautiful dwelling-place.

'The transient sufferings of today are worth nothing in comparison with that glory which will be revealed to us!

'We feel full of courage! We are constantly aware that it is much harder for you who are free than it is for us here. We never forget to remember you in our prayers. We believe that we shall soon meet with you again and that we shal again work together with great devotion and energy for the Lord and for the Church. Our trials are only for our good. Our greatest comfort is to know that you are facing difficulties with courage!

'We are with you now in spirit as you meet together. May your fellowship be blessed in the presence of Jesus! May peace reign in your midst, with love and mutual understanding!

'Troubles are allowed by the Lord so that He may make his family closer and more open to one another. He wants to see us constantly lifting our hearts to Him, knowing that we need His blessing. "Blessed are the men whose strength is in thee, in whose heart are the highways of Zion. As they go through the valley of Baca they make it a place of springs; the early rain also covers it with pools" (Ps. 84: 5–6).

'Dear friends, let none of you be downhearted or depressed. Remember—the eyes of the sinful world are upon us. We must show them Christ. Our faces and eyes must shine with joy, we must be full of inner peace!

"To live for Christ, to die with Him—
Is there a better lot to be had?"

'Pass on our greetings to the whole Church, to all, even the youngest Christian, and to all the prisoners.
'We shall remember that this time of trial for the Church will not be in vain. (Ps. 102: 19–21).
'May the Lord bless you. In the knowledge that we are with you as you meet, please sing this hymn:

"O no, there's none in earth or heaven,
Can take from us our liberty.
Let mortal flesh fear mortal bondage,
And let them fear the prison walls!

But God in love has given freedom
To spirits long in darkness held,
And freed from bonds of sin's dominion,
No man can harm our peace within!"

'Your friends in Christ: Lida, Nadya, Lyusya, Vera.'

☐

Not all young Baptists have to face a prison sentence, but there can be few for whom holding fast to their faith involves no sacrifice at all. Like other young Christians in the Soviet Union, they experience difficulty in finishing their higher education even if they are fortunate enough to gain entry to it. The Reform Baptist church in Slavgorod made a protest to the Soviet government about this on 30 January 1974. Not only are children subject to ridicule and even threats at school if they declare their belief in God, they say, but when they leave they find there is discrimination against them:

☐

'Our young brothers and sisters experience serious difficulties through discrimination in the field of education and

79

the finding of jobs. Membership of the Church is mentioned on character references and then to get into higher education or to get a job with such a reference is often a great problem. The doors of establishments of higher education are almost entirely closed to believers. The syllabuses are so constructed that to study without abandoning one's convictions is almost impossible. We have the choice: either you become a highly-educated atheist or your education remains unfinished. Such things radically contradict the Convention "On Discrimination in the Field of Education" adopted by the UN in 1960.'

☐

The story of the young Baptists involves the story of their suffering. It would be possible, indeed, to dwell more lengthily on the negative side of the picture—the way in which young Soviet Baptists are harassed and persecuted. But there is a brighter side. It would appear to be true of the universal Church that where the element of self-sacrifice is absent, Christianity falters. In spite of, and perhaps because of, the difficulties they endure, the enthusiasm and dedication of these youngsters is boundless. Convinced that the spiritual good they have received is far greater than any temporal good they may have sacrificed, they are eager to share it with others, even when laughed at or rebuffed. Their efforts are rewarded. The young Baptists are responsible for bringing more young people into the Church.

Over the past few years a number of Soviet citizens of German origin have been allowed to emigrate to West Germany. The descendants of farmer settlers of the days of Catherine the Great, the so-called Volga Germans were deported by Stalin to Siberia, but still retain their national identity and language. Many of them are Christians. Vanya Peters, born in Siberia in 1952, left the Soviet Union with his parents in 1972, and now lives in West Germany. His family moved to Latvia in 1963, and it was there that Vanya became a Christian. His story tells much about the young Baptists of the Soviet Union:

☐

'A new life began for me, full of joy and new experiences. Having received forgiveness of sins, I had the desire to tell others about Christ and also to do those things which would glorify God. On 20 September 1969, I was baptised in the river Gauja which flows near the city of Sigulda. Before the baptismal service, I told about my experience with the Lord. The elder brethren explained that on joining the Church, I would enter the path of the unexpected, which would include trials and persecution. However, I firmly believed that the God who had saved me from my sins through His only begotten Son, would also protect me in the path of following Him.

'When I was eighteen, the same brethren commissioned me to work with the young people amongst whom I had accepted Christ. In spite of the threats and prohibition of the authorities, we held a weekly young people's meeting. We read the Bible, prayed, sang, and together discussed how, and by what means, we could glorify our Lord. The authorities strictly forbade religious training of young people, but, having tasted the love of God we could not do otherwise than gather for prayer and reading of God's Word. These meetings were our very food and strength.

'We had our own young people's string orchestra and choir and would often visit other assemblies in Latvia and Estonia. The Lord richly blessed us and our ranks grew.

'In the spring of 1971, for two months I travelled in Siberia, visiting churches in Novosibirsk, in Omsk and other regions including Kazakhstan and Belorussia. What blessings the Lord let me experience! I had several opportunities to witness about Christ in the trains and other places. Some people, with tears in their eyes, would reach out their hands to me after we parted and promise to seek the Lord. On several occasions we would be confronted with atheists who with cursings and foul language would laugh at my words, but the Lord would turn this experience into blessing as well. It attracted attention and others were thus able to hear about Christ. Whether they consequently accepted my testimony, only the Lord knows, but I rejoiced that the Lord gave me opportunities to tell them about Him.

'In the autumn of the same year, I was called up to the Army, where in spite of threats and searchings by the commanding officers, my New Testament remained undiscovered. Often in the late hours of the night, I would witness to the sixty soldiers in my company. The soldiers listened many times with great interest to the Gospel, asked me questions and talked to me about spiritual things. From childhood they had been taught in the spirit of atheism, but when they heard the true Gospel, many began to distinguish between religion and true Christianity. Also, with the soldiers, we often listened together to the radio programmes and afterwards discussed what we had heard.'

□

Vanya Peters found his faith through the witness of a schoolfriend. At the age of fifteen he was taken to a meeting of young Baptists and was deeply impressed by their joy in worship. Not long afterwards he professed conversion. In his testimony he does not mention whether he had a religious home background, and clearly does not regard the matter as of great importance. Whether or not the atheists' researches are to be trusted, they do concede to the Baptists a proportion of converts from non-religious backgrounds. The story of Ivan Sidorenko, quoted in Chapter 1, bears witness to this. If Vanya Peters' enthusiasm to broadcast the Good News is representative, it would indeed be surprising if the young Reform Baptists did not win new believers.

It seems likely, nevertheless, that the majority of young Baptists were brought up in Christian homes—whether or not one accepts the propagandists' figure of 85–90 per cent. Baptist teaching lays great emphasis on the responsibility of parents to bring their children up in the faith. This evangelism in the home seems to be very largely effective. The atheist press is disturbed that the Baptists have prevented the drift of adolescents away from the Church.

The atheist booklet *Children and Religion* (Leningrad, 1970, p. 20), cites a set of rules recommended to parents in the upbringing of their children in a Baptist newsheet called the *Children's Herald*. Children are expected to:

'1. Love Jesus Christ with all your heart.
2. Pray, kneeling down and with your eyes closed, not less than three times a day.
3. Go to meetings where the Lord is worshipped.
4. Always be gentle and obedient.
5. Make friends only amongst children who love the Lord, and do not take part in worldly games.'

Atheists often criticize the Baptists for being killjoys, making their children's lives a misery. But they have to admit that they do an effective job in protecting young minds from the pervasive influence of atheism. A writer in *Science and Religion* (no. 3, 1967, pp. 62–65) reviews some of the Baptist literature on children's upbringing:

□

'Here are a few thoughts from the *Instruction to Parents*: "'A person will be most meek and god-fearing if he is first trained by the right upbringing; if he is given no such training, or the wrong sort of training, he will be the wildest beast of all those that roam the earth' (Plato) . . . From his very birth a child should be present (in his mother's arms) at family prayers and times of singing. As he grows up he may stand, and then kneel for the prayers . . . The influence of parents on their children begins much earlier than many people imagine. What is learnt in the first seven years will be remembered for the rest of a person's life, and what is learnt between seven and fourteen will be remembered for half his life, and what is learnt between fourteen and twenty only for about five or ten years."

'The authors of the *Instruction to Parents* are terrified that freethinking ideas may penetrate the childish mind: "Do you know what is going into their minds during the day? They may have received some ideas from a pagan or anti-religious world-view which will be death to their souls. What are you giving them to counteract this?'

'One must admit that the authors of this little booklet are far-sighted: they fully realise that all the circumstances of our life, and especially study at school, will make atheists of children, and are anxious to make convinced believers of them long before they start school.'

The same article tells how Baptist children are trained to stand up for their faith at school and even to evangelise their schoolmates:

'The letter entitled *Children are the Future of the Church* calls on parents and others involved in the instruction of children to take a stand against the Soviet school. The author of the letter angrily berates those who "foolishly" abandon "adolescents and young people to the hands of the devil so that they are ruined in body and soul . . . Every year we lose several tens of thousands of souls". The letter demands that children should be taught religion so that a five- or six-year-old child can prove to his peers in the play-ground that God exists, so that children "should be courageous in battle . . . especially at school, where even in the first class they are told to renounce the name of God". The author states directly that children "are often helpless to withstand all the cunning methods and admit defeat; but those who while this is going on study the Holy Scriptures may even be strengthened through the battle, amazing by their steadfastness the most powerful lecturers, teachers and journalists, who employ all their strength to convince them".'

☐

While the responsibility of bringing up Christian children is laid squarely on their parents, the Church evidently plays its part. As well as the personal teaching of Sunday schools, there are periodicals for children which *Science and Religion* mentions without explaining exactly where they come from. For the youngest children there is the *Kindergarten*, intended to be read aloud by parents. Older children who can read themselves have the *Children's Friend*. Both contain short tales with a moral to them, and the latter includes questions to study on the content.

Where individual churches are able to organise children's activities, it is not on the scale that Western Europeans would describe as a 'Sunday school'. Children may gather in small, informal groups in ordinary homes, of necessity unobtrusively. Fyodor Basko, from the village of Kalorashovka in Moldavia, was one Baptist who organised children's meetings. He has ten children himself—already almost enough for a class! It was the presence of his own children at the prayer-meetings of the registered church to which he belonged until 1963, which led to friction with the leaders of the church. Basko left and founded an unregistered church, along with a few other like-minded people. The Council of Prisoners' Relatives' *Bulletin* (no. 11, March 1973) tells his story.

Soon Basko was involved in the organisation of children's meetings in the village, and for this he was arrested in 1967. Returning home in 1969, undeterred, he became still more active in this work. He became pastor of the church, his home became the meeting-place of the congregation and here meetings were held for children too. In February 1973 criminal investigations were opened against him, he was arrested a month later and sentenced to two and a half years.

Once again the pattern of the Reform Baptists' work amongst young people is etched out. They see the need for the younger generation to be taught about Christ, they are determined to do it but their work leads to consistent and bitter opposition from the State. The Berdnik family in Kaliningrad are another example. Their five children were removed from their parents and taken into the care of the State after it was found that they were being brought up as Christians. Part of the accusation was that the children had been allowed to attend a children's meeting on Saturdays. The description of the lessons is from the prosecution documents, reproduced by the Council of Prisoners' Relatives in their *Bulletin* (no. 10, 1972):

☐

'It was established that the Berdniks had allowed their children Leonid and Nikolai to go to lessons in religion and prayer meetings at the homes of Gelis, Sulin and Berdnik, where they were taught the fundamentals of religion, to recite poetry, sing psalms and simple religious music. During the lessons the children became familiar with and learnt by heart religious dogmas, such as the songs, "Be careful, little mouth, what you say", "Our Father gave us salvation", "Stand for the truth of God, children", "The arena stained with blood," etc. Much of what the children were taught was recorded on tape, and their lessons were checked on by believers at their illegal meetings, which encouraged the children to attend. Children were attracted into the group by other means too:

(*a*) by setting the children religious questions emphasising the virtue of submission;

(*b*) by preparing special cards with questions on religious themes;

(*c*) by attracting children to attend meetings of adult believers and using them for the teaching of religious dogma.

'The children's meetings were held separately, generally on Saturdays, from 1968 on.'

☐

The Berdnik children were taken out of their parents' custody so that they could be brought up in a spirit of atheism. The youngest at the time was only a baby, less than a year old. This is the worst thing the authorities can do to a Christian child, and while a number of cases have come to light in recent years, there is no reason to suppose that it is a frequent occurrence. Orthodox children have suffered the same fate. The Reform Baptists, however, appear to arouse the fiercest persecution from the authorities, since their whole organisation is outside the law. In spite of their frequent appeals to the State to allow them the Constitutional right of freedom of religion, their worship and even their family life continues to be disrupted. From earliest childhood a member of a Reform Baptist family has no protection from arbitrary repression.

In education, in career prospects, and most of all in their church life the Reform Baptists suffer disadvantages. Yet they are known as the 'young Baptists'. The trials of this Christian life have no power to repel believers. Far from it. Here is an extract from a poem, this time coming from young people in a registered Baptist church, but expressing the satisfaction of being a Christian, compared with all the attractions of secular life:

□

'Not all that gives us pleasure brings us profit,
Nor does all that gives us pleasure do us harm.
But joy alone can hold no lasting goodness,
The fleeting dream leaves only tears behind.

So, all that is not helpful we'll abandon,
We will not spend our time and strength in vain,
And all that hides the seeds of sin and anguish,
We'll leave behind, to burden us no more.

The road before is one without a turning.
Before us lies the blessed promised land,
And in our hearts the voice of God is ringing
And calling us to be with Him in peace.

Our dream is not in vain, but is more wondrous
Than pleasures which will pass can ever be:
The door to our salvation has been opened
By Jesus Christ who loves eternally.

Our joys are pure, are full, are satisfying,
Are all our souls could ever want or need;
We say without pretence or shame or falsehood—
"Dear friends, the Christian life is good and free".'

IVAN VASILIEVICH MOISEYEV died on 16 July 1972 at
Kerch in the Crimea.[1] A twenty-year-old conscript to the
Soviet army and the son of a village family, he was a
member of a Reform Baptist congregation at Slobodzeya in
Moldavia. Moiseyev was no ordinary Christian, and for
this reason he deserves a chapter to himself. His experience
of God was extraordinary to those who knew him during
his lifetime just as it is to us who read of it after his death.
At the same time Moiseyev's dedication and strong desire
to preach the Gospel wherever he might be is shared by
young Reform Baptists all over the USSR.

The Council of Prisoners' Relatives devoted the whole of
their *Bulletin* no. 9 to Ivan Moiseyev's life and death. The
material reproduced here is largely taken from this source.
Another version, in the devotional *Herald of Salvation*,
differs slightly in some respects, and where this gives a more
detailed account the editors have used this version. Most of
the story is in Moiseyev's own words. On his last home
leave he made a tape recording of events up to that time,
which forms the greater part of this chapter. The last few
months before his death are seen through his letters home.
Only the final days have to be told in the third person.

The details of Ivan Moiseyev's death are not fully known,
although his death certificate stated that he died by drowning

[1] For further information, see *Vanya*, by Myrna Grant, Victory
Press, Eastbourne, 1975.

in the Black Sea. From the marks on his body it was obvious that he had been tortured before his death. All attempts to make him renounce his faith in Christ and agree to refrain from his evidently successful evangelism had failed. Whether his torturers intended to kill him we shall never know. If by doing so they meant to injure the cause of Christianity they undoubtedly failed. The final part of this chapter is devoted to some of the many letters which were written to his family by young people, both Christian and non-Christian, who read about Moiseyev's life and death. That the authorities were deeply concerned at the impact of these documents is shown by the press campaign which followed, with article after article attempting to explain away the facts and attribute it all to an anti-communist plot. Furthermore, a number of trials took place of Christians who had distributed the Moiseyev documents: among them was that of the Latvians Petrov and Kolesnichenko mentioned in the previous chapter. Another Reform Baptist, Nikolai Khmara, who died in prison under torture in 1964, is still remembered as a martyr of the Reform Baptist Church. Vanya Moiseyev has become the martyred hero of its young people—and even of the young beyond its ranks.

□

BRIEF BIOGRAPHY OF I. V. MOISEYEV (from the *Bulletin*, no. 9, 1972)

Ivan Vasilievich Moiseyev was born in 1952 in the village of Volonitrovka in the Suvorov region of Moldavia. His parents were believers.

His father, Vasili Trofimovich, and his mother Ioanna Konstantinovna had eight children—seven sons and one daughter—who were brought up in the knowledge of Jesus Christ. Almost all the Moiseyev children gave their lives to the Lord's service.

In 1968 Vanya finished secondary school and the same year, in the Slobodzeya Evangelical Christian and Baptist Church, he turned to the Lord with repentance and received salvation in Christ. Six months later he entered into the divine Covenant through Holy Baptism in water, and became a member of the Church.

From the time of his new birth he had a burning desire to witness to Christ. In the last few months before his call-up to the army he trained as a driver and worked in this capacity, first at home and then during military service. At the same time he preached the Gospel with great joy in the church and amongst the young people.

In November 1970 brother Vanya was called up for military service. The first few days of his service were a harsh testing of his faith in, and devotion to, the living God. His prayer-life took on a special power, and God strengthened him to be a greater witness to both soldiers and officers, most of whom were deeply hostile to the young Christian and subjected him to terrible persecutions and tortures. While suffering extreme torments, one day he prayed all night, and in the morning saw a heavenly choir of angels descending, singing a hymn:

'In every corner of the mourning earth,
 In every place, wherever people dwell,
 There flows a mighty, pure and joyous stream,
 A stream of faith, the call of the Good News.'

This hymn became his favourite song until the day of his martyrdom on 16 July 1972. To his last breath he remained a faithful witness to the Truth.

According to one of the officers, 'Moiseyev died a hard death, he battled against death, but he died a Christian.' This reminds us of the words of the Roman Centurion on Golgotha, coming willy-nilly from the lips of a pagan, after the death of Christ: 'Truly he was the Son of God!'

Praise be to the Lord, who has taught faithful followers of Jesus how to die for His name! In his young, short life and martyrdom Ivan Moiseyev glorified Christ.

□

THE TAPE RECORDINGS
'God filled his short life with signs and visions', the

Bulletin states, 'through which Ivan was strengthened, but the officers were stricken with fear, for the supernatural manifestations of the power of God were seen by all.'

Prayer

When I arrived at my unit, I first of all looked for somewhere to pray. I found one room which was empty until ten o'clock in the morning. An officer worked there during the day, but until he arrived, nobody used it. Reveille was at six. I would get dressed and go there and pray until breakfast. The soldiers did physical jerks and drill, but I would pray for two hours. Sometimes I was even late for breakfast because I had not looked at the clock.

Two months went by like this. The day came when my faith in the Lord was to be tested. God showed me how I should act. That morning I got up at five and prayed until nine. Around nine o'clock, I hurried to roll-call; everyone was there already waiting and looking for me. I had to explain to the company commander why I was late. He had already been told that I was a believer. The major ordered me to fall in and said I would be punished.

Our conversation was continued later on the practice-ground (it was at Stary Krym). The soldiers were working at their combat training, but the officer and I were discussing quite another matter. He wanted me to renounce my beliefs. When we got back to the barracks, I was again called up to see the commander and several officers talked to me. They gave me a punishment: to work all night. I worked joyfully, singing and praying. Next day I worked again. The soldiers had drill to do, while I had to wash the barrack floors. The barracks are large, and I had a scrubbing-brush and soap. I did it willingly and joyfully. The officers noticed this, and as soon as I started scrubbing they began calling me to see first one, then another, until I had seen them all in turn. Finally I was called to see the top officer of them all—the divisional commander. It was his political assistant who saw me and we had a discussion lasting about three hours. At first he just shouted at me but after a while

91

he stopped. I asked him, 'May I say something?' He agreed, thinking that he had already convinced me and I would listen to him. But I was listening to God all the time, not to men. I told him, 'It is no use shouting, you will not frighten me by shouting at me.' Then he drew up two chairs and suggested we sit down. He began to talk less roughly, and eventually, realising he could do nothing, he left.

After this they sent me to a different unit where the colonel talked to me all day. Twenty days later we drivers were sent on a five hundred kilometre march. Then we were sent to Kerch.

The first trials

There they began to put me to the test. The first trial: for five days I was given nothing to eat. 'Have you ever been ill?' they asked me. 'No,' I replied, 'I haven't, and I've never been in hospital either.' They thought that after five days without food I was bound to fall ill. But I didn't. The first day I felt quite normal, and the rest just the same. Praise God! I wasn't ill because I prayed. They checked up on me and took x-rays—and I wasn't ill. So they let me go. The officers heard about this and said 'Give him something to eat, otherwise he'll get us into trouble, if he dies of hunger!'

I didn't go to drill, nor sing their songs.

Then they tested me another way. It was winter by this time. There was snow on the ground and thirty degrees of frost. While the soldiers were asleep in the barracks they would take me outside and order me to stand in the frost for five hours. I was in summer uniform: just a shirt, trousers, boots and cap. They didn't care how I spent the time, so long as I spent five hours outside. I would pray the whole time, however long they gave me, whether it was all night, one hour or two. After this they would call me in and ask me if I'd changed my mind. Then they would repeat the punishment. But I never even felt the cold. If the officers went outside just for ten or twenty minutes, they would start shivering with the cold. They would look at me in amazement because the frost didn't affect me. Sometimes I was out the whole night, and even several nights in a row. This went on for two weeks. After that they decided to let me sleep in the barracks with the other soldiers.

Caught up by an angel

I remember the first night they let me sleep in the barracks after being sent out in the frost, I had got undressed and went to bed after lights-out at ten p.m. I was already asleep along with the other soldiers, when suddenly an angel appeared to me and said, 'Ivan, get up!' I thought it was a dream. I got up, but don't remember how I got dressed. We flew out of the barracks, not by the door or window, but the ceiling and the roof opened before us and we flew away to another planet. The angel said to me, 'On this planet you must follow me, because you don't know the way.' I agreed and followed him. We walked through long grass and came to the banks of a stream. The angel crossed the stream but I was afraid. 'What are you afraid of?' he said. 'Snakes,' I said. 'Follow me and don't be afraid. It's not like earth here —there are no snakes.' So I crossed over to him. Then he showed me John, one of the disciples of Christ. John was the first person I saw. He flew to me and told me, the angel interpreting, what their life on that planet is like. The light there is brighter than daylight on earth, but there was no sun to be seen. Then, after John, the angel showed me the prophet David, Moses, and then the prophet Daniel. I didn't talk to them, but the angel did, and told me what they said.

When we had gone further, the angel said, 'We have come a long way, and you are tired.' We sat down beneath a large tree, and rested a while. The angel said: 'I want to show you the heavenly city—the New Jerusalem. But if you really see this city as it is, you will not be able to stay alive, and you still have a lot of work to do on earth. We shall fly from here to another planet, and I shall show you just the light of this city, so that you may live and know that there really is a New Jerusalem.' We flew to another planet where there were high mountains. There was a deep gorge between the mountains. The angel took me down into the gorge and said, 'Look up,

93

and you will see the light of the city.' I looked and saw a light, brighter than the sun. Even an oxyacetylene lamp would look dull beside it. I thought I would be blinded, but the angel said, 'Don't be afraid, you can look and nothing will happen to you.' So I looked . . .

Then the angel said, 'It is time we went back to earth.' So we flew back. I remember the barrack roof and ceiling opening and we landed on the floor. For a second or two the angel stood on one side of the bed and I stood on the other. Then the guard on duty in the barracks called 'Reveille!' The lights went on and the angel disappeared.

All the soldiers got up. I looked at my bed: it was made, and I was fully dressed. I could remember clearly everything the angel had shown me.

The man in the next bed got up (he is from Moldavia too, from the village of Oloneshty), and asked me, 'Where were you all night?' I had thought all this was a dream. 'Don't you remember how I undressed and went to bed when you did?' I answered. 'Yes, you did go to bed when I did, but some time after three o'clock you went off somewhere, and I thought you'd slipped off into town.' 'Let's go and ask the sentry on duty,' I said. So we asked the sentry. 'No-one went out last night,' answered the sentry, 'I was standing by the door.' Then I told everyone about my flight with the angel and where I had been, but they didn't believe me.

For two days I had a strange feeling of not knowing whether I was living in heaven or on earth. I worked with the lorry as usual, but this feeling remained with me—I couldn't believe I was on earth. Later this passed. But the wonderful revelation of God still amazes me. The story of how I had been caught up by the angel to heaven went round the whole unit. And at once the officers began working on me again. Fifteen or twenty times a day I was called into various departments—but God was with me in a wonderful way.

The Sergeant's leave

Often I was called to headquarters where they talked to me, interrogated me, threatened—all so as to re-educate me and prevent me from having any free time. If I was called ten times in one day it was nothing. Sometimes they called me fifteen or twenty times.

One day our company met for political instruction. To begin with there were about twenty people there. For some reason, the company commander, who was supposed to take the session, didn't arrive. So the soldiers decided to have a discussion on the subject of the difference between my God and their God. They asked me:

'Who is your God?'

I replied, 'My God is almighty and all-powerful.'

One sergeant, an Armenian from Yerevan, said to me:

'If your God is almighty, and if He is alive and can do anything, then let Him make me go home on leave tomorrow. Then I'll believe in Him!' All the soldiers agreed:

'Yes, if God lets him go, we'll know that God really exists. Unless he does, we won't believe anything you've told us is more than a fairy-tale. If your God does this, we'll believe that He is a living God and can do anything.' I prayed in my spirit, and the Lord told me:

'Say that I can do this.'

So I turned to the sergeant and said,

'Tomorrow you will go home on leave, but first you must do as I say.' He was smoking. 'Throw away your cigarette,' I said. He threw it away. 'Now take the packet out of your pocket.' He took the packet out and burnt it.

While this discussion was going on the whole unit of 150 men had gathered round. Then our officers came and sent us about our duties. In the evening I met the sergeant and we talked most of the night. We only got about two hours sleep. He promised that he would believe. I gave him some advice on how to behave on the way and at home. His parents are unbelievers and know nothing about God. He hadn't even spoken to his officer about going on leave.

In the morning, immediately after reveille, I was sent in the van to fetch some provisions. Afterwards I was told that a high-up officer, some general or other, had telephoned our unit from Odessa and ordered that this sergeant should be sent home on leave immediately, in ten minutes' time. But I believe it was not a general, but an angel, who telephoned. At headquarters they made out the documents and the sergeant went on leave. When the soldiers heard about it they told the officers how we had spent our 'political instruction' meeting the day before, and how everything had turned out 'as Ivan predicted'. The officers sent some soldiers after the sergeant to bring him back, and so contradict the general opinion of the soldiers that Ivan's God had sent the sergeant on leave, but they were too late. The sergeant was already on the train and they could not catch up with him.

When I got back to the unit the soldiers gathered round me and joyfully told me that he had gone. I didn't have time to talk to them before being called to headquarters. There the major-general, the divisional commander, was waiting for me. He asked me what had happened, so I told him everything, in order, about yesterday's political meeting . . .

'But how could you know he would go on leave?' asked the general. I replied that God had done it.

Evidently by order of the general they wanted to take me away from this unit and send me somewhere a long way away, but the soldiers stood up for me. They all left their work and gathered at headquarters. So I stayed with my unit. After these lessons in 'political instruction' we were all sent out East for the harvest. I wanted to wait for the sergeant to come back from leave, but they sent us out East.

□

While he was working in the East, brother Vanya said, the Lord sent him two visions for a confirmation of his faith. One of them he saw at night, coming out of a tent. A bright ribbon appeared in the beautiful starry sky. 'I couldn't read it for the bright light,' Vanya said, 'so I started to read letter by letter, like a child in the first class. It said, "I am coming soon".'

From Vanya's letters we learn: 'When the sergeant came back from leave and I returned from the East, there was a general meeting of the unit where I was ridiculed and threatened for preaching. They tried to explain away the incident about the sergeant's leave, but the sergeant came forward and said:

'Whose power did this? Now I believe that it was God, because you refused to let me go on leave, but God did a miracle for all to see.'

'All the soldiers were triumphant and the officers had to go away in disgrace.'

☐

My healing[1]

From the East we were sent to the village of Zhosten in the Odessa region. I had to drive to the station of Zatishe. On the way my lorry broke down. I decided to uncouple the transmission. It was ten o'clock at night. With a tool in my hand I lay down under the lorry. When the universal joint came free, I had time to fling myself to one side, but fell under the back wheel, which rolled forward on to my right shoulder and chest. The lorry with its load weighed six tons. I just had time to shout, 'Reverse gear!' Two soldiers were standing nearby. I couldn't breathe, but could see the soldiers struggling for ten minutes to start the engine. They succeeded, moved it back and I crawled out, stood up and fell down again unconscious.

They took me to hospital at Zatishe, but there was no doctor to be found. I was feverish and my right arm hung limply, as if it were dead. They took me straight to Simferopol and put me in the military hospital. They took x-rays.

On 26 November 1971 my temperature went up to 107°F. They proposed a major operation: amputation of the right arm and half a lung. At supper-time in the ward I got out of bed and started praying out loud in front of all the patients.

---

[1] The next two paragraphs are entirely from the *Bulletin* version, since the other here drops into the third person and appears to be an enlargement by the compiler on what was actually on the tape. This version alleges that it was three days before Ivan reached hospital, but his own story appears to contradict it.

When I had finished, I went to sleep, very much tormented by the fever.

The next morning I woke up at six o'clock and found I was lying on my back with my arms behind my head. I looked at my left arm, and realised it was normal; I looked at my right arm, and couldn't believe it . . . I thought it was a dream. Slowly I moved my arms around. My right arm didn't hurt! I felt I could breathe freely and easily. I took two deep breaths. What was this? I got out of bed, felt the bed. Was I really awake? I did some exercises. I could breathe freely!

Then I began to pray and thank the Lord. But I still couldn't believe it was real. I thought it was a dream, and went back to sleep.

The doctor came on his morning rounds. They told him something had happened to me, and he immediately came over to me. He wanted to take my temperature.

'I don't need a thermometer,' I said. 'I feel quite well.' But I let him take my temperature to prove it. Then he said, 'Take your medicine.' 'Your medicine doesn't help,' I answered. He looked at me, frightened, thinking I'd gone out of my mind.

'I knew you couldn't cure me,' I said, 'so I turned to my Heavenly Doctor. He healed me during the night.'

The doctor was even more bewildered. So I got up and took the thermometer (I also wanted to know what my temperature was). It was normal, 98·4°. I didn't take the medicine. The doctor was amazed, and went away.

They called me to the doctor's office. The house-surgeon, a lieutenant-colonel, asked me: 'What happened, Moiseyev?' I told him all about my healing. They all knew already that I was a believer, and understood which Doctor I was talking about. The surgeon opened his record-book and said:

'Look, this is the treatment we were going to have to give you: amputate your arm and throw it away, because it was completely useless, and half your lungs were useless too; you were to have had this operation today. For the first time in my life I have seen a miracle. There really is a God, and He has healed you, because we could never have done it!'

During this conversation two other doctors were with him. They discharged me straight away. He wrote everything down in my medical book, gave it to me, and I left. After the hospital I had to go to headquarters to collect my documents. There were about two hundred soldiers there who had been with me in the East, and all our officers. When they saw me they were all amazed that such a thing could happen—I was walking out of hospital five days after such a serious accident! When I told them what had happened to me in hospital, they believed that God exists.

They gave me my documents and travel instructions, and I went to the bus station. Suddenly a car drew up. The military driver got out and called me over. In the car was the colonel—the chief surgeon for the Crimea, who had been called specially for my operation. When he heard that the operation had been cancelled and I had been discharged from the hospital he was most alarmed. The doctors who met him had told him about my healing, but he could not believe them and immediately came to the station to find me and bring me back. But he was too late. I told him briefly how the Lord had healed me, showed him my arm and my chest, and he let me go and left me in silence.

So I went back to my unit at Kerch, where many people had heard about me. All the soldiers were amazed to hear about my miraculous healing.

Trials began again. As usually happened, after a manifestation of God's power in me, Satan raged and tried to do all the evil he could. I was constantly called to various departments for interrogations and threats. As always I used to pray and sing hymns on the way to the headquarters. Once I was singing as I walked across the park. It was a clear winter day. Suddenly I saw a bright light shining in the blue sky. A shining star began to come down from the sky, and as it got nearer, it grew bigger and bigger. Then I saw it was an angel. He came down quite close, but didn't reach the ground—he stayed about two hundred metres up. I walked

99

along the path to headquarters, and he walked in the air above me. He said to me: 'Ivan, go on and don't be afraid, I am with you.' He walked with me right to the door of the headquarters, then disappeared. I believe that he was there in the room, but neither I nor the officers could see him. But I could feel the presence of God, and felt no fear of the trials I had to suffer.

Two or more months ago, before they sent us on a long expedition, I prayed all night. At three or four o'clock in the morning God comforted my soul by showing me a heavenly choir who sang, 'In every corner of the mourning earth'. While the angels were singing this song I saw them—they were all in shining, many-coloured clothes. When they had gone the Lord told me, 'This is to comfort your soul. To-morrow you will leave this place.' And so it turned out.

I am reading from the book of Numbers, 22: 31—'Then the Lord opened the eyes of Balaam, and he saw the Angel of the Lord standing in the way, with a drawn sword in his hand; and he bowed his head and fell on his face.' So in those days God sent angels to believers. And in the same way today He can also show angels to all those who believe in Him, and reveal His power! I want to read again in Mark's Gospel, 14: 35—'And going a little further, He fell on the ground and prayed that, if it were possible, the hour might pass from Him.' So, dear brethren, this is what hours of testing, the difficult hours, are like. There are hours like this for many of us. Jesus Christ prayed at such a time. He knew everything which awaited Him, but we don't know anything. I want to invite you to pray. Just as Jesus Christ prayed, let us now bow our knees and pray to the Lord. (Prayer.)

The miracle of the bread

Once I was driving a van full of bread. The loaves were loaded in trays. The back doors were locked with two bolts and a padlock. A sergeant was riding with me in the van, in charge of the bread. As I drove I heard a voice, 'Slow down.' I could not understand why, so I drove on. Again the words

100

came, but for some reason I did not obey. I looked at the speedometer: it said sixty k.p.h., and I thought, that's not much—why should I slow down? Then suddenly I saw a loaf of bread rolling along the asphalt at the same speed as the van. I was surprised, and suddenly realised, 'God is stopping me.' I brought the van to a halt. The sergeant and I got out and looked at the van. The doors were shut with the same bolts and padlock. We opened the door and saw that half the bread had gone. Looking up, we saw our bread lying on the asphalt. The sergeant was very surprised indeed, and said, 'Vanya, come here and tell me who closed the doors. We did it together, you see all the locks are in place but the bread has gone. I've been working with this van for six years and such a thing has never happened.'

I realised that God had stopped me and that He knew what lay ahead. We picked up the bread and forty or fifty minutes later were ready to go. 'Let's go on,' I said to the sergeant, and soon saw the answer to the question why the bread had gone. Not far on, at the first crossroads, there had been a bad accident. A bus which had overtaken us while we were picking up the bread had collided with a mobile crane. Passengers had been killed. We should have been killed in that accident, but God stopped us. I praised God because, as He said, 'I am the God who keeps you,' and so He had done.

We arrived at the unit. The sergeant told everyone about what had happened, but they did not believe him. Then the officers called me and interrogated me again. I explained: 'God saved our lives through the miracle with the bread. He loves us all and is ready to save even you, even from eternal death, which awaits all who do not accept Jesus Christ.'

My arrest

Then the military tribunal arrested me. I was taken to headquarters at Simferopol for an inquiry by the Military Prosecutor. They told me there under which article I was to be sentenced: the punishment was from three to seven years.

'We have decided,' said the Prosecutor, 'to give you seven

years. I'll give you three days to change your mind. If you don't renounce your God, you'll get seven years.'

After the inquiry I was taken to Kerch. Three days passed. I was taken to the prison. Again they threatened me, 'You'll have to stay here.' The same day they took me away again and once more gave me 'three days to change my mind'. This time went by too, and they came and took me to Odessa. There too they tried to frighten me. They made me stand with my leg in a sort of refrigerated chamber for five minutes. My leg froze and my boot became white. I couldn't stand on that leg, it was so completely frozen. It hurt a bit. Then I started praying, and my leg got better again. Once again they gave me three days to consider and took me back to Kerch.

When this time was up, the Prosecutor said, 'We shall meet again in the court-room.' They came for me and told me they were taking me to Simferopol. They put me on the Simferopol–Irkutsk train, which had a prison carriage. We were automatically guarded. We arrived at Simferopol. I asked, 'Where is the trial to be?' They answered: 'It's a military tribunal who will try you. Even if there is a trial your parents won't come, nor anybody else. And we'll sentence you to seven years. You'll go there and you'll stay there seven years. So think about it: which is better, two years in the army, or seven years in prison?' I said, 'Let them give me seven years.'

They took me to a big prison with stone walls two and a half metres thick. I was there ten days. Every day I was in a different cell. Of course I was in solitary confinement. For instance, in one cell there was a bench, and you could stand or sit. In another cell there was a bed, you could lie down and it was dry. In the third cell there was icy cold water trickling from the ceiling. The next cell was refrigerated; it was freezing cold—you could really freeze there—and so on.

They made me wear a rubber suit and put pressure on. They were trying to see how long a man could hold out. They tried it out. 'Well, have you changed your mind?' they asked. Then they put the pressure on again. But already they could see that it was unendurable, and they let me go. Ten days passed like this. The officers said, 'You'll be here for seven years!' I answered, 'If it is God's will that my place should be here, then I'll be here seven years, but if not I'll be taken away tomorrow.' So it happened—after ten days I was taken back to Kerch.[1]

□

[The last period given to Vanya to change his mind expired on 16 July. Since he remained true to the Lord, that afternoon, the commander of the regiment, V. V. Malsin, with a group of people in plain clothes, ordered Vanya to follow them in his own car. According to eye-witnesses, they drove to the place of execution in a 'Pobeda' car.

By their hands, our dear brother Vanya was killed.

On 19 July, when the body of their son was given to the parents, eye-witnesses of Vanya's death, 'expressing their sympathy', said, 'Moiseyev did not die easily, he fought to the end, but he died a Christian.']

□

FROM VANYA'S PERSONAL NOTEBOOK
REMEMBER, Vanya, all your life,
REMEMBER! How you saw angels for the first time in your life when you were fifteen years old.
REMEMBER! How you walked along and there were snakes beneath your feet, but you walked firmly and were not afraid. You walked a long way before you overcame the biggest snake, but you overcame it because Christ helped you.
REMEMBER! The vision, when you stood on guard with the angel on a great cliff and watched the sea. When a storm arose on the sea and a boat sank, you leaped into the sea at the angel's command and pulled to the shore as many of the people as you could save. The waves roared,

---

[1] Evidently the story is not complete. Vanya must have been granted the home leave during which he made the tapes between this episode and the final torture.

threatening death. But when the last one was brought to the shore you fell, exhausted, but *remember* how the angel took you and set you on the cliff again to renew your watch.

REMEMBER! How Jesus showed you how much work there was to do on earth, how so much was lying fallow and how you must husband this land.

REMEMBER! When you were tired on the way to an interrogation, and an angel came down from Heaven and said, 'Vanya, do not be afraid, I am with you.'

REMEMBER! The fiery notice in the sky: 'I am coming soon,' and the fiery banner and what was written on it. Know that God forbade you to tell that to anyone.

REMEMBER! How it was in prison when they were preparing to burn you, that you saw all this.

REMEMBER! How for two days you did not know whether you were living in the body or out of it, after you saw the light of the Heavenly Jerusalem, and how happy you were with the angel.

REMEMBER! That prayer is the best link with God.

REMEMBER! Your family, your father, your mother, your seven brothers and your sister.

REMEMBER! Whom do you love more, your family or Jesus Christ? And that you have not yet given the whole of your strength for Christ.

☐

IVAN'S LETTERS

15 June 1972

Christian greetings, dear parents! I was very glad to receive your letter. I want to tell you that I am well, through the goodness of our loving Father. I wrote to you when the Lord revealed to me what is the best way, and how all Christians should be. I will write you all about this in another letter—the Lord reveals all things.

My dear parents, when I was at home Ilyusha taught me some Psalms. Please write them out for me. And Ilyusha, learn some more Psalms and teach them to the older people so that they can sing, because they don't know them. Yesterday I went to church at Kerch and met some local brethren from another church, an unregistered one like ours. There was a brother from Sochi, and they knew of me. It was very good to meet them. All the local people and those from Sochi send greetings in the Lord to all the brethren in Moldavia.

My dear parents, the Lord has revealed the way to me, and I must follow it. I have decided to follow it, but I don't know if I will ever return, because the battle was harder than it was at first. I shall have more and harder struggles now than I had before. But I am not afraid. He will go before me. I only pray that my beloved parents may not suffer. I love Jesus more than myself, I obey Him, though my body is a little afraid, or doesn't want to go through with it. Because I do not value even my life as much as Him. I shall not expect my own will to be done, but the will of the Lord. He tells me to go and I go.

Do not be sad if this should be the last letter from your son. Because even when I see and hear visions and see angels and hear them talk, I am amazed and cannot believe that it is Vanya, your son, who is talking with angels. For he, Vanya, was also a sinner, but through suffering the Lord has washed his sins away. And he does not live according to his own will, but according to the will of the Lord.

I am writing again to those who do not believe in our Lord Jesus. We call you anti-Christ so that you know, even though you do not believe, that it is the Lord who gave me life, because this body was dead. I want you to know, Semyon, my dear brother, that the Heavenly Father will give you life too. Even I have grown weary of telling you this. Much time has passed and I am far away. I want even you, Semyon, to know that the Lord exists. I tell you, if you will believe it, that I have spoken with angels and have even flown with them to another planet, where eternal life is waiting for us. Believe it if you will—you who do not yet know of this other life. I am writing to you because I have seen all this.

I greet you all in the great love of Jesus Christ. Your little brother in Christ, Vanya, is writing to you.

I can still write you this letter freely, to tell you that after the joy of meeting Sergei there was not just one storm but several. I rejoiced about everything: when there is no storm, not even a breeze, it becomes monotonous—I am so used to storms!

Oh, how beautiful and wonderful it is there, far from our earth! What joy there is there! Oh, brothers, let us all go forward, do not be afraid, when you have to pass through fire to reach the heavenly goal.

If in your heart you love anything more than Christ you will not be able to follow Him.

Now let me tell you what kind of bodies angels have—and ours will be like them if we are faithful unto death. I wanted to see angels and I did, I saw how they are dressed and I told you about it. But their bodies are not like ours. Their bodies do not prevent you from seeing beyond them. You look and you can see through them, as if through glass. Inside and outside, they are pure, pure as crystal or a mirror. And you can see everything within them too. There is not one sin, not one error. Some day we too will receive spiritual bodies like that. Such bodies can see everything, Jesus and the angels and the Heavenly Father, and we shall know each others' thoughts too. Oh, what joy, what purity and what love there is there. How clean and pure they all are: if you were to polish glass it would still be dirtier than those bodies.

I am impatient for your reply. May you all go on towards the heavenly country.

No date

Peace to you, beloved parents. Some brothers in Christ from Zaporozhe have been to see me. I am glad, even though they are from the registered Church. They betrayed me last week because I was preaching Christ.

Despite the fact that I am a soldier, I am working for the Lord, although I have difficulties and trials. Jesus Christ gave the command to proclaim the Word of Life, in the town, in every church, in the unit, to the officers and the men. I have been to Divisional headquarters and in the Special Department. It was not easy, but the Lord made it turn out well, so that I preached His word even to the most senior officer. I was oppressed still further and then sent away.

Those who live not according to the will of man, but that of God, will be saved. Keep the commands of Jesus. I will tell you later of the many miracles and revelations I have seen.

In the Lord,
Vanya.

9 July 1972

You will soon receive no further greetings from your son, but although I am weak, I greet you now with the love of Jesus Christ and the peace of God. I have been forbidden to preach Jesus, I am suffering torments and trials, but I have told them that I shall not stop telling the news about Jesus. The Lord put them to shame before the whole unit. They were testing me, and the soldier who went on leave stood up and told them all about it, and asked, 'Whose power was that?' But they did not want to let me go. They did shameful things. They asked me why one tree was green and another bare, because there were two trees side by side, one green and the other bare. I asked them what the difference was. They replied that there was a great deal of difference—one was alive and the other dead. So I told them that this was the difference between a believer and one who opposed Christ. That put them all to shame.

There is much work to be done, and I am following the command of Jesus. The trials are great, and the torments are not easy to bear. I have a lot to tell you, but I cannot write it in letters. I am waiting until I can meet with Sergei and carry out the command of Jesus. May we not be ashamed to speak about the Lord now. They all see the miracles and say 'There really is a God!'. I will sow and I will go forward, as the Lord teaches me through the Holy Spirit and the angels.

Do not be offended, but I am trying hard to do this work. And you know that it is not easy for the body. I go to church here, although it is forbidden. The brethren send greetings to everyone, and I send greetings to everyone in Slobodzeya and Yermoleyka.

I long for Syomya and Galya to believe and see the power of the Lord and that He really exists. Here all the officers and soldiers are saying that God exists, and they are afraid because they see His miracles and His power. I wish Grandmother too would come to believe and see that the road she is on leads to Hell. Jesus Christ is calling you while there is time, and He will give you eternal life. I cannot give you life. Believe the Gospel.

In case you should hear that I am not free any more, I have left a little notebook here in Kerch where I have written about the miracles. Maybe you can come here, or someone will bring it to you—the Lord knows about that. Be faithful Christians. He will strengthen you and give you power. Ask, for He is rich towards everyone and will give you freely all you desire.

I will not forget you in my prayers.

In the Lord,
Vanya.

11 July 1972

Greetings in the love of Jesus Christ. Vanya is writing you this letter. I am very happy for you—we may be able to meet just once more. Let me tell you that leave has been strictly forbidden me. But I am working for Christ with all my might; I do not want to boast, but just want you to know and not to forget me in your prayers.

On 10 July in the evening, one soldier repented while I was preaching Jesus Christ. I was very glad, and still greater power filled me.

I have not yet managed to meet Sergei. Praise God for everything. If I do meet you, I shall tell you everything in detail, but I cannot write it.

When I look and see how fiercely the sea rages,
How terrible the waves which break above our heads,
Nevertheless joy and courage fills my heart,
Because of You, who came back from this battle,
Because You came back to us with victory,
The fearful crushing waves defeated,
We too shall come back to the shore,
We too shall come back with victory.

You will have days when dawn never comes,
And service will be full of difficulties
And the bitterness of partings.
Can times be easy when terrifying storms are raging?
When it seems that weary brothers will be drowned?
But no, the Lord will send His mighty power
And hope, the strengthener of our wills.
And however costly it may be
You will fulfill the holy command of the Father.

You will share your last ounce of strength with a brother.
You will give your last ounce of strength for Christ.
You will obey the hardest of commands
Though you are tried by the sea many times.
You will serve as you are commanded,
Though it is hard for you,
You will fulfill the holy will of Christ!

I do not think you will see me again ... and if you are
thinking of coming to see me, there is no point. I will not
forget you in my prayers. I shall try very hard to meet with
Sergei. Perhaps I have already completed my final task.
Warmest Christian greetings to you from Vanya, your little
brother. Greet everyone. I do not expect an answer, and
please do not write ... Goodbye, God be with you, dear
friends. When I think of you I feel sorry for you, but I
remember one thing: I go to fulfill the command of Christ.
Greetings from Vanya.

15 July 1972
A letter to his brother

I received your letter, little brother, and am late in answering it because there has been a very harsh storm, because they found the postcards and literature at Sergei's and confiscated them.

Do not tell our parents straight away. Tell them: Vanya wrote me a letter and said that he is going into battle at the command of Jesus Christ. It is a spiritual battle, and he does not know whether he will come back.

I send you all, dear friends, old and young, one verse: 'Be faithful unto death, and I will give you a crown of life' (Rev. 2: 10).

Accept what may be the last greeting on this earth from the least of your brothers, Vanya.

☐

A LETTER FROM THE MOISEYEV FAMILY TO THE GOVERN-MENT OF THE SOVIET UNION

On 16 July 1972, while serving in the ranks of the Soviet army in the town of Kerch, our son and brother Ivan Vasilievich Moiseyev died from terrible tortures for his faith in God.

Wounded, tormented by the tortures inflicted on him, but still alive, he was forcibly drowned in the Black Sea at a depth of 156 cm—his height was 185 cm. This was done in the presence of Lieut. Colonel V. V. Malsin.

The death certificate stated that the cause of death was 'Mechanical asphyxiation as a result of drowning'. A report on examination of the body says 'Death occurred as a result of violence inflicted'.

On 17 July 1972 at eight a.m. we received a telegram saying 'Your son has been tragically killed, inform us of your arrival'. Having travelled to Kerch, we decided to bury him in our home village. We were shown the face of our son in the coffin, and then the zinc coffin was sealed. Our son Semyon was with us, a member of the Komsomol, who was called into the office alone by the officer and talked to him for a long time about something Semyon would not tell us about.

Captain V. V. Platonov, the officer in charge of short-term service, and a private soldier were detailed to escort the coffin to Volontirovka and take part in the funeral. The coffin was brought to the village on 20 July. On receiving the coffin with the body of our son, we decided to look at the body and photograph it.[1] So we began removing the solder around the edges of the lid of the coffin.

Captain Platanov and the officer, who were sitting there, saw this and at once became uncomfortable. Saying, 'We must leave, we're in a hurry', they quickly got into the car and disappeared. When we opened the coffin and began to remove the clothes and look at the body, Semyon forcibly prevented us from examining the body to photograph it, telling everyone to 'photograph it dressed'. On the body those present saw six deep wounds around the heart, which had been made with a pointed instrument. On both sides of the head were grazes and cuts, the legs and back had been violently beaten, there were large burns on the chest and bruises around the mouth. All this was confirmed by 23 witnesses, residents of Volontirovka, in a statement dated 20 July, 1972, which we enclose.[2]

V. V. Malsin, the Commanding Officer, told us in the course of conversation: 'On the morning of the 16th I was busy—I had to talk to a group of civilian visitors. After lunch Moiseyev and I drove to the beach in the car.' According to onlooking soldiers Malsin drove in one car with some strange civilians, and Moiseyev followed alone in another. They went off to an unknown destination.

[1] It appears that the family did not suspect foul play until they actually saw the body. Visitors have since reported that the mother, hysterical with grief, insisted on dressing the body in civilian clothes, and for this reason the coffin was opened.

[2] These villagers—not Christians so far as is known—later withdrew their statement under pressure from the police. Press articles reported their withdrawal.

'Moiseyev died a hard death' said Malsin, 'he fought to the end, but he died a Christian.'

On 19 July 1972 when the body of Moiseyev was handed over, Malsin said: 'I am on my seventh packet of cigarettes today.' On 1 August he said, 'My wife lost fifteen kilograms in a week over the experience of Moiseyev's death,' and that 'he would not use the car he drove'.

☐

So Moiseyev died. Remarkable as his ministry had been during his life-time, the witness of his death has been still more powerful. Hailed as a martyr, he has become a saint for the young generation of Christians, and the story has spread both in the unregistered and the registered Baptist Churches, giving inspiration and a new encouragement to the spirit of self-sacrifice for the Kingdom of God.

The concern this has caused to the Soviet government has been reflected in the press, and indicates the extent to which they are anxious to suppress the truth. A series of articles appeared in various papers in the nine months following Moiseyev's death, all claiming that he died from accidental drowning, and that his relatives invented the story of his torture out of malice against the Soviet regime. The trial of some Baptist ministers accused of preaching and spreading the information has been reported in the press. Christians' homes have been searched for any literature about the case, and this is confiscated when found.

Further reports—not confirmed by official sources—say that the town of Kerch and the village of Volontirovka were sealed off to visitors for a time and that the unit of which Moiseyev was a member has been dispersed. The officer responsible for his death, Lieut. Colonel Malsin, is reported to have suffered the loss of his child, and his wife has had a nervous breakdown: he is said to be convinced that the judgement of God is pursuing him.

In spite of the measures taken to suppress the effect of Moiseyev's life and death, however, he 'though dead, yet speaks'. His parents have been greatly comforted in their bereavement by the many letters they have received which bear witness to the fruit of their son's life. Here is a selection from them; they were published by the Council of Prisoners' Relatives in their *Bulletin* no. 11 (March 1973).

□

THE LETTERS

From soldiers Lyosha, Alexei, Valerik, Misha, of
Bobruisk (Belorussia)

'We are keeping a vigil of prayer . . .' In a moment of silence we honour the martyrdom of our dear friend and fellow-soldier Vanya . . .

Although we have never seen each other we are alike washed and born anew through the blood of Christ, and for this we always give thanks to Him.

In August we had already heard about brother Vanya's martyrdom and we felt the blow as no-one else could, since we are in the same position, wearing the same uniform, living amongst the same people and like him looking forward to the long-awaited return home to our parents— which he did not live to see. Our hearts are heavy when we look at our suitcases standing ready to be picked up in a few days' time as we say 'Hello, mother!' For him that day did not come, though his was the best reunion of all—reunion with the Lord.

We long to comfort you, although it would be impossible. We long to stand by your side and take all the pain upon ourselves. We know that this loss is more than you can bear. Many people have already given you comfort, and we believe that Vanya's angel has not left you to this day, but comforts you day and night. He wipes away your tears and carries up each tear to Heaven. And when you meet God, where He sits on His throne with His Son and the twelve Apostles, the Church, and the angels, He will embrace you and wipe away your tears forever. Surely it will be soon.

The Enemy tried to kill Vanya's soul, hoping he would renounce his beliefs, but God defended his soul and so the

Enemy flung himself on his body in merciless fury and tore the breath from it. The Enemy thought he could close Vanya's mouth, but never dreamed that hundreds of others would thus be opened.

Yes, the valiant warrior's mouth is closed, but our mouths are not closed. We shall continue to bear tidings of salvation to all the dying. We tell everyone how God manifested His power in miracles, and how Vanya was pitilessly killed—we cannot be silent. 'For having the same spirit of faith as he who wrote, "I believed, and so I spoke", so we believe, and so we speak' (II Cor. 4: 13).

Many people listen to us eagerly, and now that we have the *Bulletin* to give them they are still more interested, take it home and show their neighbours. We believe that many mouths will be opened. Already it is not we who speak to the officers, but the workers, who have read about it and seen the photographs. We talk to the soldiers too about the power of God and the faithfulness of His children. If the Enemy closes our mouths too, then others will arise. They may punish us and take away all we have on earth, but they cannot tear the freedom of Christ from our hearts.

Almost every evening we go into the garden together to pray. We receive much from the Lord and see His hand upon us. When we heard about the deeds of our friend and brother Vanya, and about his martyrdom, we were still more strengthened in our prayers. The vigil of prayer which Vanya held has not been abandoned: God has set our hearts aflame and with the help of God's encouragement we shall carry on a vigil of prayer in the Army. May the Enemy know that God's work is set on a firm and eternal foundation and our desires will never destroy it. We are keeping a vigil of prayer.

We soldiers go out to the place where we pray in the evenings and, in a moment of silence, we honour the martyrdom of our dear friend Vanya, who gave his life for Christ. We bear the sorrow in our hearts, we are grieved that the Enemy should take the lives of the true children of God.

We are forbidden to pray, to meet together, our Gospels

114

have been confiscated in the hope that we will be re-educated, but by doing this they have made the fire grow stronger. We are not forsaken but have much Bread.

Dear family, do not be cast down. God has done a great work in the salvation of souls through your dear son, our brother, friend and contemporary Vanya. He followed the way, not listening to the counsels of flesh and blood. Jesus gave him the command and entrusted him with the banner which he was to carry through fire and tempest. Vanya fulfilled the command and was able to report its completion. Now eternal glory awaits him, and the reward of his loving Father.

God will surely reward you too, dear father and mother. You brought up your son in the Spirit and in Truth; you aroused in him a thirst for fellowship with God.

'Behold, the longed-for eternal life soon
You will exchange for this life's dreary path,
And you who so much suffered for your Love
The angels will with greater splendour crown.'

From brother Kolya, Kirovsk

Before I was called up to the army I knew little about Christ. In the army I heard nothing about Him. After my demob. I did get to hear a lot about Christ, but I did not in the least want to believe and accept Him. But Christ Himself called me and I thank my Saviour Christ, for He did not abandon me to this dying world.

After military service I was active in the Komsomol, keen on sport and the leader of the Komsomol group at my place of work. I was all set to go to college. But when Christ called me to serve Him, I surrendered my Komsomol card, stopped my sporting activities, and the door of the college was closed to me.

But I thank my Saviour Jesus Christ for His love for me, for now I am saved through the blood of Jesus Christ, and have eternal life. Praise and glory be to Christ my Saviour!

Yes, our dear brother in Christ, Ivan Moiseyev, has left an example for us of how we should live, fight and die!

Our dear brother Ivan will be forever in our hearts. He bore many torments, sufferings and tortures, but he was faithful to Christ to the end. He has left us an example of how to win the crown of Christ.

I am twenty-three years old. Until this year I lived a worldly life. I ended my military service and returned home. My mother is a believer, but not my father. She often talked to me about Christ, but I did not accept Him because I loved worldly pursuits more, and the world seemed more interesting than Christ. But mother did convince me that I should leave the world and serve Christ. She prayed to Christ for both of us and He heard her. One night I saw a vision, I saw Christ, who was calling me to His service. A short time after that, Christ again appeared to me in a dream. Now I am Christ's servant and I give Him thanks for everything, because He did not abandon me to this sinful world. Praise be to Christ for His love for us all!

From sister Nadya, Kiev district

When I read the journal where Vanya's brief biography was told, and the miracles which happened to him, and his last days, I was deeply moved.

I admire his steadfastness, the strength of his love for Christ, his self-sacrificing spirit, his readiness to renounce his life in order to show that God exists, and that He is almighty and all-powerful.

Vanya wanted only the best for people. He expended all his energy in order that they might repent, he preached Christ crucified. He was all love and purity, and wanted others to become just as pure before the Lord. But alas! They did not understand or accept him! How stupid and cruel were his murderers! They martyred Vanya in the same way as his beloved Jesus Christ. Dear Vanya! How cruelly he suffered . . . But at the same time he is so happy. Now he lives in the Heavenly Kingdom, far from this sinful earth. There love and peace alone rule. I too long to be like Vanya and, if it should be my lot, to die like him, continuing faithful to Christ.

And now I beseech the Lord that He will teach me to pray and serve Him as Vanya served Him, my brother in Christ.

From Masha, Kirov district

I live out in the wilds and so only recently heard of the deeds of brother Vanya. I hope and believe that his life and martyr's death will bring forth fruit a hundredfold, and will bring new life to those Christians who are sleeping, and that many, many more young people will come to Christ in repentance, swelling the ranks of the Christian youth. I believe in almighty God; He is able to do this here too. In our village there are just my two sisters and myself who are believers.

From Lubya, Fergana

. . . Vanya has become for us young people a symbol of faith, hope and love. We have realised that we should give our youth—the flower of life—wholly to the Lord's service, and if the Lord should even take it away for ever, then we should assent without hesitation and do as Vanya said . . .

We have our own copy of the *Bulletin* about Vanya, with the photographs, and it is always left where it can be seen. When we meet with troubles we are always comforted by looking at the portrait of Vanya. He looks at us with such a penetrating glance, as if to ask, 'Friend, are you able to go through this life as I did?' And then you have to fall on your knees and say 'Lord, give me the faith to imitate him as he did You!'

From Galina, Lvov district

When I read through Vanya's story, I was filled with joy for him, because he did not falter before the Enemy and the Enemy did not see him broken, but faithful to God to the end.

I did not weep, but sang, sang the youth hymns, 'We greet you, the new generation of Christ', 'In every corner of the mourning earth', and 'Wonderful land'. I rejoiced and still rejoice that we have such good examples in our brothers and sisters, who deserve the golden crown.

From Lyuba, Rovno district

I am two years younger than Vanya. I am also a member of Christ's Church. I believe that Vanya's deeds will inspire and strengthen all those who come to know about them, old and young. Through Vanya many will come and bow before God.

I have no father. He is alive, but does not live with us, so I only have mother. But I thank the Lord very much, because she is a believer. When I was small she prayed for me and implanted in my heart the sacred promise; the Lord has called me to His path. I thank Him and rejoice because He has changed everyone and everything for me.

Looking at the photograph and reading about him, I shall be inspired always by his faithfulness and readiness to obey Christ.

Not only Christians have reacted positively to Ivan's story. His parents received letters from unbelieving and un-committed people who had also felt the impact of the power of God in his life. Here are some of them.

From Rita, Altai region

I read about your son in the *Bulletin* with deep emotion, and could not refrain from writing to you. At present I am not a believer, but I want very much to be like Vanya ... I cannot even think about his terrible death without emotion. I want so much to be like him. He loved Jesus Christ very much, indeed he loved Him more than anything else, but how is one to attain such things? It is all amazing, and he is my hero whom I take for my example. Forgive me for writing like this, but I cannot help myself. Rita.

From Maria, Volyn district

I am unknown to you, but please accept my respects. Forgive me for troubling your hearts with my letter. I live in the village of Galina Volya, I am an ordinary farm girl. There are a lot of believing people in our village. So it was that I chanced to read in the journal about the dreadful death of your son. Of course I am not a believer, but when I saw it I could not be indifferent . . .

May the Lord be with you. Maria.

From Leonid Alexandrovich, Brest district

I heard about your grief and what happened to your son Vanya moved me deeply. I still cannot believe that such things can happen in our country. I feel ashamed at the behaviour of your son Semyon, Vanya's brother.[1] I have a sister who is a believer, but if anything like that happened to her, I would not for anything behave the way Semyon did. Please tell him this.

Forgive the shortness of my letter. Goodbye.

☐

Creative writing too has been stimulated by Moiseyev's story. In Russian Baptist circles it is common for poetry to be read during the meetings, and the young martyr has become the subject of some of these poems. For a final comment on his death and its effect on young people, this verse, while perhaps not immortal poetry, sounds a heartfelt note of grief and inspiration:

☐

Again the children stand around the grave;
Christians encircle it, and bow their heads.
This, our last duty to one dear to us,
We take our leave of brother, son and friend.

[1] A letter from Semyon was published in *Altai Truth* on 9 June 1973 asserting that his brother's death was an accident. Semyon said how glad he was to have lost his childhood faith, and that Vanya had almost been persuaded by him to stop believing! He blamed the Baptist leaders, not his parents, for the 'slanderous tales' about his brother's death.

The parting is untimely; our hearts grieve
To see you whom this world no more will see.
We stretch our hands to you, we whom you loved—
Farewell, you servant of the living Christ!

Beloved of God, counting this world as dross,
With loving heart and truth upon your lips,
Tested by evil, suffering fearful pain,
Yet you did not deny your Master's name.

In icy winter, standing in the night,
You prayed to Christ, who held your spirit up,
And warmed you with the blood of Golgotha.
You did not shrink—and winter lost its sting.

Though troubled and tormented and confined,
You never ceased to tell the news of Christ.
They burned your breast with irons; but your heart
Burned stronger than the fires of torment could.

Still in the pain and grief you sang God's praise,
Though gripped in irons, though wet by icy streams,
They pierced your flesh and dragged you to the sea,
Hiding the guilty traces of their crime.

Yet even then He went with you—the Christ;
Down to the shore where you were dragged to die.
All Russia hears the sound of your young voice;
The waves are echoing your funeral hymn.

Only your mortal flesh the murderers killed,
Only your heart the cruel blade could stop,
The sea's depths cannot bury your young soul,
Nor can the work of God be stayed by death.

The mother for the last time holds her son,
Tremblingly kissing forehead and shut eyes.
No, not these sacred tears of love and grief—
A mother's tears—will warm your flesh again.

Blessed are you, young warrior, death's fresh prey!
You were a faithful watchman at your post.
Many are those you helped to conquer sin
And bring their lives' sweet spring to serve the Lord.

So in the fray a brother's heart is stilled,
The pulse of life has ceased for ever more,
The gentle voice he raised to God in prayer
No more in earnest supplication sounds.

But on that day when Christ shall come for you
And make you drink the water crystal-clear,
He'll greet you as a conqueror, praise your deeds,
And seat you on the throne that waits for you.

The throne is yours indeed—the throne of God!
Amen!

ON 14 MAY 1972 a student, Romas Kalanta, burned himself
to death in the city square of Kaunas, Lithuania's second
city. He was a Lithuanian nationalist, protesting against
Soviet domination of his small nation. He was also a Roman
Catholic, like the majority of the Lithuanian population.
The day after his death riots swept the city as people demonstrated how deeply they sympathised with Kalanta's action.
This was no isolated incident, but an open manifestation of
the groundswell of resentment at the Soviet annexation of
Lithuania thirty-five years ago. The Catholic Church has
become a rallying-point for the Lithuanian nation, and as
nowhere else in the USSR the younger generation is swelling
its ranks. A reaction against Soviet power and its alien
ideology perhaps; but the evidence suggests that these
young Catholics are sincere in their faith and prepared to
suffer persecution for it.

When, in 1939, the Soviet Union annexed Lithuania as
part of Stalin's pact with Hitler, the Catholic Church was
beginning to suffer the same fate of diminution in an increasingly secular society as the Church in the rest of
Europe. Soviet power came with its atheist education for
the populace and repressions against the Church, and the
trend away from the Church was actually reversed. Now,
90 per cent of the population is Catholic. Unable to carry
out massive closures of churches as elsewhere in the Soviet
Union, the authorities have sought to starve the Church of

priests by limiting the theological seminary to an intake of twelve students per year. Even these are carefully vetted by the Council for Religious Affairs. They have not succeeded, however, in providing the Church with leaders who will not protest at the repression of religion. Some, indeed, have given in to pressure, but many priests have consistently refused to obey government restrictions on, for instance, the teaching of children. Some, like Fathers Zdebskis and Bubnys in 1971, have been imprisoned. The laity support such men, and themselves have carried on a storm of protest against the authorities, especially since Kalanta's death in 1972.

1972 saw the birth of the *Chronicle of the Lithuanian Catholic Church*. In three years sixteen issues have reached the West, each one filled with detail about the life of the Church. Its second issue concerns a petition, the *Memorandum of Lithuanian Catholics*, dated December 1971. Addressed to Mr Brezhnev, it was signed by 17,000 people, and claimed that more would have signed if the security organs had not prevented them. In spite of attempts to silence them, the Lithuanian Catholics have gone on to more protests. Young people and children have been one of their major concerns. In March 1973 a protest about atheist education in the schools and the right of parents to bring up their children in whatever faith they wished was signed by 14,284 people, of whom a quarter were schoolchildren.

The Catholic Church in Lithuania has great strength, and at the same time it is experiencing fierce opposition. Perhaps because the authorities fear nationalism even more than they fear religion, a great deal of effort has been put into trying to wean people away from the Church. Naturally the young generation is the chief target of these attacks. For most of them, opposition is centred around the school. Nevertheless, for the most part their resistance has been strong.

The *Chronicle* devotes much of its space to events concerning children, and indeed since issue no. 14 it has begun a regular section entitled 'In the Soviet school'. Issue no. 11 included a historical survey of the schools' progress in atheist education since the Soviet takeover. One incident demonstrates the strength of Catholic loyalty which the atheist educators had to contend with in the early days:

☐

'In 1940, when Lithuania was newly occupied, the Soviet authorities first turned their attention to the schools, and tried hard to make them atheist. They immediately forbade prayers before and after lessons, and took down the crucifixes from the classrooms.

'In one secondary school in Panevėžys the headmaster ordered the caretaker to collect the crucifixes from the classrooms and destroy them. But the children barred the caretaker's way.

' "We won't let you desecrate our crucifixes," cried the children.

' "I am only doing what the headmaster told me," replied the caretaker. But the children took the crucifixes, shared them out amongst themselves and took them home.

'In the engineering school in Panevėžys a teacher told the girls to take the crucifixes down off the walls, but not one of the pupils would do it.

"What cowards you are," said the teacher angrily. "You, Suveizite, you're a Komsomol member, show the others an example and take down all the crucifixes in the classrooms!"

'The girl turned pale and burst into tears.

' "Teacher, my conscience will not let me do it."

'That day no-one touched the crucifixes. The next day Soviet soldiers took the crucifixes down and threw them out of the window into the street. People picked up the desecrated crucifixes and kissed them.'

☐

The situation remains little changed to this day. Unlike other parts of the Soviet Union, where a believer at school may be alone in a class of atheists, in Lithuania the teachers wage a lone battle against whole classes of Catholic children who are prepared to stand up for one another. The *Chronicle* (no. 7) tells of eight-year-olds being made to copy drawings making fun of their faith:

☐

'On 25 May 1973 the little second-formers were told to sketch caricatures making fun of their religion. Many, failing to understand that this was wrong, sketched away. However, others were scandalised at such behaviour on the part of the teachers. One girl said, "It was so terrible that I could not look. I asked permission to go to the lavatory, and stayed there half an hour, just so as not to have to do the sketch." '

☐

Like Christian parents in other parts of the Soviet Union, Lithuanian parents do not like their children to join the Communist Youth Organisation (Komsomol) or its junior branch, the Pioneers. So worried are the authorities by the low membership that they will go to any lengths to make children join. Bribery by promises of good school marks, cajolement or downright force have been used. The *Chronicle* (no. 7) again:

☐

'In 1966, Miss Medeigyte, a teacher in Ceikiniai, desiring to enlist all of our children in the Pioneers, gave the pupils a written Lithuanian-language exercise, so that children might learn to write their application for membership of the organisation. When the pupils had completed the applications—as an exercise in Lithuanian composition—the teacher, gathering up the papers, told the children, "Now you are Pioneers!"

'Mrs Šiaudinienė, a teacher in Ceikiniai, drove Algis Sapiega out of a student residence into the night for not joining the Komsomol, and for attending church. The boy travelled home seven kilometres by night in a temperature of 25°F., and with a blizzard raging. When he arrived home he fell ill.'

☐

There are many more examples, of students expelled from colleges, of lowered marks and so on. Most young people, however, still refuse to identify publicly with the Communists by joining the Komsomol. The *Chronicle* (no. 5) states that reluctance to join is growing, whether from religious or patriotic feelings, or from sheer indifference. A specialist in atheist education, B. Bitinas, in a book entitled *Religious Students and their Re-education* (1969, p. 128), says the *Chronicle*, writes that a Christian upbringing is the most frequent reason why Lithuanian youngsters are not joining the youth organisations. Some Catholics do join, but are liable to be criticised for church attendance. The *Chronicle* states firmly that 'Young Catholics in Lithuania realise increasingly that membership of the Komsomol is a great mistake.'

Nor is the atheism thrust at children in school having a great effect. Most of them are firm enough in the faith they are taught at home and church to be impervious to atheist teaching, which is often crude and shallow, relying on caricature rather than on reason. The *Chronicle* (no. 7) reproduces the words of a fifteen-year-old at a school where the corridors are hung with posters making fun of the church:

☐

'If the atheists are unable with the militia to drive people away from the church, then like a worm they gnaw at their souls ... Children are drafted into the Pioneers and other organisations ... How painful that among our dear Lithuanians are murderers who kill the souls of innocent children, leading them down wrong paths ... In the school show-case is the following note: "People seek a road to heaven because they wander off the road on earth." It is the drunkards, the hooligans, who have strayed from the path. Those who are looking for a way to heaven always control their passions, are always orderly, do no harm to others, and thus seek eternal life. The arrangers of the show-case clearly demonstrate their inability to think right. One must think out one's ideas, in order not to make a fool of oneself ...'

☐

Still more revealing of the situation is the remark of a mother whose son refused to join the Komsomol, reported in the same issue of the *Chronicle*. Asked by a government official why she had not allowed the boy to join, she replied, 'I don't see a good example among the Communists. They are liars, since they themselves secretly go to church services, but smear others.' What better description of the strength of the church and the weakness of the Party! Clearly Communists and atheists are regarded with intellectual and moral contempt.

Well able to stand up to the authorities in school, young Lithuanians have also carried their faith and their love of their country's traditions into public places outside. Romas Kalanta's death is still remembered. On its first anniversary, in May 1973, students and other young people went to lay flowers on the spot where he died, in spite of the streets being crowded with police and security men. For a brief instant, the *Chronicle* (no. 7) tells us, the old national flag of independent Lithuania flew above Kaunas city hall. So afraid were the authorities of fresh demonstrations that numbers of young people were taken out of the city for the day by their schools.

A few days later, the eighth issue of the *Chronicle* tells us, a demonstration of a different kind took place, symbolic both of the spiritual and national aspirations of the Lithuanian young:

□

'In Lithuania there is a famous hill at Meškuičiai called the Hill of Crosses. At one time it was covered by traditional Lithuanian shrines, but the atheists desecrated the sacred place many times, tearing down the crosses and burning them. However, people would always replace the shrines on the hill, so dear to the heart of every Lithuanian.

'The Hill of Crosses had just about recovered from damage suffered during the devastation of 1961. However, at the end of April 1973, it was once more devastated; not a sign of the crosses survived. The desolate, denuded hill seemed to be waiting for believing hands and loving hearts once more to crown its desecrated head with the symbol of the Redemption.

'At midnight on 19 May 1973 an unusual procession appeared at the edge of the city of Šiauliai. A small group of serious young men and women prayerfully carried a cross. They went quietly, meditatively, praying the Rosary. From time to time the cross, measuring nine feet nine inches and weighing ninety-nine pounds, would be transferred from the shoulders of one to those of another. The cross was decorated symbolically: a heart pierced by two swords. On the handle of one sword was a swastika, and on the other a five-pointed star.

'Lithuanian young people were carrying a cross not in quest of health, but in atonement for the desecration of the cross, and in reparation for the sins of our nation against the Redeemer.

'They carried the cross also as a symbol of victory. The night of 19 May, many knew of this procession with the cross and devoted an hour to prayer and the veneration of the cross. During that hour, many, with hands joined in prayer, carried the Cross of Christ in spirit.

'All the cross-bearers received Holy Communion the evening before. As preparations were being made for the Way of the Cross, it was discovered that someone had informed the state security people about the project.

'Security agents travelled along the proposed route throughout the night, from Šiauliai to the Hill of Crosses. To the cross-bearers, the success of the procession seemed a miracle.

At 2.30 a.m. on 20 May 1973, the Hill of Crosses boasted a beautiful new cross. Around it were planted flowers, and a candle was lighted before it. Everyone knelt and prayed, "Christ our King, may your kingdom come to our country".

At 6.45 the sound of a car was heard. The security people rubbed their eyes. All night they had been chasing after the cross, and here it was! Angry hands tore the cross down and hauled it off. But by noon, another cross stood in its place. The more the atheists destroyed them, the more the crosses seemed to sprout from the ground.'

Some of the young people who were involved in this demonstration were interrogated by the security police the next day, but although they were threatened with punishment, no-one was arrested. The *Chronicle* goes on:

'This persecution on the part of the security organs not only failed to intimidate people, but even inspired them with courage. One woman who carried the cross wrote: "Lithuanians, be aware of your strength! It lies in Christ and in our unity with one another! Stand immovable and courageous, on guard for what is sacred and dear to your hearts! Do not let them desecrate the Hill of Crosses. Do not leave it lying bare. Take your joys and sorrows, your hopes and victories there; take your love of God and your loyalty to Him there: carry your cross to the Hill of Crosses!"

'The desecration of the Hill of Crosses had inspired a new idea: if it is impossible to erect a cross on the Hill of Crosses, let us begin erecting crosses in our yards, in our homes, in our own hearts, and in the hearts of others.'

□

This erecting of a cross, as it were, over the Lithuanian nation is something very dear to the hearts of the people. Their opposition to the Soviet power and longing for the freedom of the nation is closely linked with their struggle for religious freedom. Lithuania, in spite of official intolerance, is a more Christian country than many in the West. Its Catholics hope that one day the Church may be restored to its rightful position of respect in the community, and in this hope they educate their children. The tremendous solidarity of the Lithuanian Catholics gives hope that they will continue to resist the atheism which so small a minority has yet embraced.

'ON 4 APRIL 1972 the headmaster of my school, Nikolai
Nikolaevich Daigot, called me out of my lessons, and took
me to the children's department at the police station. Then
a policeman arrived, and some other people including my
father. The policeman took me by the arm and made me get
into a car. They took me to the children's home at Krasnaya
Sloboda, not far from Soligorsk. When they took me I cried
a lot . . .

'Surely they don't have laws in this country which say that
children should be taken away from their parents? Like all
children, I want to live with my mother. Because I and my
mother believe in God they are robbing me of my childhood
and are always questioning me: first the headmaster, then
the newspaper reporter, then the procurator. But I shall
never become like my father or like the people who put me
in the home. And if they take me away from my mother
again, I shall run away again so that they can't do it.

'Please help me and defend me from these wicked people
who don't love me and don't want me to be happy.'

□

The writer of this emotional appeal is Seryozha Supruzhevnik (Seryozha is the Russian diminutive of Sergei),
fourteen years old at the time and the child of a broken
marriage. His father, evidently a ne'er-do-well, had deserted
Seryozha's mother for another woman. When he petitioned
for a divorce the court considered him unfit to have custody

130

of the child, but also rejected the mother's claim and ordered the boy to be taken into care. The reason: she is a believer, a member of the local Reform Baptist community, and wanted Seryozha to be brought up as a Christian.

Seryozha's mother takes up the story:

☐

'Seryozha could not bear this humiliation and ran away home. For this I was fined fifty roubles and threatened that if Seryozha would not return to the children's home, they would take him further away so that I would not be able to see him at all. The Procurator of Soligorsk, Comrade Livunok, threatened to deprive me of my parental rights, and told me that all my complaints would get me nowhere, since nobody was going to enter into discussion with me and since people who believed in God were only second-class citizens. The Deputy Chief of Police of Soligorsk, Comrade Sokolov, told me that they would confiscate my flat and make me move out of town. And these were not empty threats. For three months already I have not been given the documents for my flat (since the alteration of my identity after the divorce), and this in spite of the fact that my other son Alexander, who is on military service, is living in the flat too.

'Not for anything does Seryozha want to return to the home. I too want to live with my son. It is my legal right. There is not a civilised country with laws which deny a mother's right. The laws of this country also uphold this parental right . . .

'I have already forwarded a complaint to the government, but my complaint was passed on to the Supreme Court of the Belorussian Republic, and the vice-president of the court, Comrade Shardyko, replied to me: "It has been proven that you involved your son Sergei in a Baptist-Evangelical sect, and took him to meetings of the sect. In the interests of your son Sergei the court rightly decided to place him in the care of the welfare and medical authorities." '

☐

In November 1972 Seryozha's mother was in fact deprived of her parental rights and sentenced to three years' imprisonment for her active part in the Baptist community. 'Surely they don't have laws in this country which say that children should be taken away from their parents?' asks young Seryozha. His own experience has answered his query. Soviet law allows for the deprivation of parental rights by the courts in cases where parents are said to be having a bad influence on the children, or are otherwise unfit to bring them up. Religion can be such a 'bad influence'. The Soviet law *On Marriage and the Family* states that:

'Both parents or either one of them can be deprived of parental rights if it is established that they are deviating from the fulfilment of their obligations in the upbringing of their children, or are misusing their parental rights, treating the children cruelly, exerting a harmful influence on them by immoral or anti-social behaviour, or alternatively if the parents are chronic alcoholics or drug-addicts.'

Realising its importance in the formation of its future citizens, the Soviet state lays great emphasis on the role of the family in the upbringing of children. Not only must it be a stable, happy place, but must play its part in the education of Communists and patriots. A leading article in the newspaper *Ukraine Truth* on 12 June 1974 speaks of the State's care for the physical well-being of its young citizens, and continues:

☐

'Within the all-encompassing care of the government for our children, the family has been, and remains, the prime educator of the young. It is in the family that the best qualities of the Soviet man are nurtured—devotion to the ideal of Communism, a high degree of conscientiousness, diligence, and an imperishable love of the Motherland . . .

'The family is the cradle of our society, where, alongside the nursery school and school itself, the world-view of the adolescent is formed and his preparation for working life takes place. The role of parental example is enormous . . .'

☐

The Soviet press has of late laid great emphasis on the role of the family in the upbringing of good Soviet citizens—perhaps because it is disturbed at the lack of enthusiasm of many young people for Communist ideals. Here again is a leading article, this time in *Soviet Latvia* of 31 May 1975. It speaks of the co-operation of family, school and state:

☐

'The family, the school and society as a whole must do all they can to help our wonderful Soviet young people to acquire a secondary education, to study and understand in greater depth the best interests of our country, the goals of our social development, to develop the ability to work well and to attain the reality of our ideals. Only on this path will the younger generation find a place for itself in society and attain personal happiness.'

☐

Acting according to this credo, the Soviet state considers that it has every right to remove a child from a family where God is revered above the ideals of Communism and loyalty to the Church is taught alongside love of the Motherland. The Supruzhevnik family is not by any means the only one to suffer in this way. The Berdnik family of Kaliningrad, whose five young children were removed in 1972, have already been mentioned in chapter 4. On 22 March 1975 Ivan Muzyka protested to the General Procurator of the USSR and other high authorities that he had been threatened with the loss of his ten children, aged between one and fifteen. On 13 April he was given an ultimatum: renounce your faith within one month or your children will go. The best documented case of all is that of the Sloboda family, from the village of Dubravo in Belorussia. In March 1970 the father of the family, Ivan, wrote this account of their conversion to Christ and their subsequent experiences:

☐

'Amongst the forests of Belorussia, in a remote corner of the Vitebsk district of the Verkhnedvinsk region, lay the village of Dubravo. The light of Christ had not penetrated

133

there and there was not a single believer in the village. Among others there lived the family of Ivan Fyodorovich and Nadezhda Stepanovna Sloboda. In 1965 a relative came to stay with us and brought a copy of the Gospel. She suggested we should read it, but we were afraid and refused. But the Lord stirred up Nadya's spirit and one night when everyone else was asleep she got up, took the Word of God from her relative's pocket and began to read it. This happened several times. I too read it with her in secret, and then we began to read openly. Members of our families gathered in our house to hear the reading of this divine Book. We had radios and began to listen to religious broadcasts. The Lord gave us a spirit of repentance and twelve of us turned to the Lord and received new life. Our lives changed. This was soon noticed and then persecutions began: stones were thrown through the windows of our homes, the electricity was cut off, so that we could not listen to the broadcasts, doors were smashed in as people broke into the room where we read the Word of God, I was expelled from the collective farm and lost my allotment of land. But our faith only grew stronger. There was not the slightest doubt that the Gospel was the truth, when we read the words: "They persecuted Me; they will also persecute you", which was what immediately happened to us. My brother Vikenty, now in prison, was sent to reconvert us, but he heard the Word and changed his course. His wife was also opposed to him, helped to persecute him, and did not want to read or listen to the Gospel, but one day as she listened to the radio at home she repented and was converted. The fire of the Holy Spirit had already caught in four homes . . .'

☐

Ivan and Nadezhda had five children, and in the spring of 1966 the local authorities decided that they should be removed from their parents' influence. On 20 April, after a court hearing which had taken place in February, the two elder girls, Galina, then aged eleven, and Alexandra aged nine, were taken away to a children's home. For two years the children were kept in appalling conditions. Their hair

134

had to be shaved because of lice and the elder girl's feet suppurated from the damp. Letters from their parents were kept from them. Finally they could bear it no longer, and on 4 January 1968 they ran away and arrived, half frozen, at their home.

Their parents take up the story in a protest written to Mr Kosygin in March 1968:

□

'Two days later the matron of the children's home and an official of the Verkhnedvinsk district arrived, intending to take the children away, but the girls climbed on top of the stove with loud wails, begging not to be taken away. No attempt was made to remove them forcibly from their parents' home and, threatening us with the police, the visitors left.

'The next day the same people came again with a police officer, Lebed. When they were ordered to put their coats on, the children clung to their parents and the house was filled with a terrible wailing, this time of all the children in the house. The policeman, unable to stand the children's noise, went into another room and ordered me, the father, to go to the district police-station.

'... From 19 January to 21 February this year, the children went to school, but then on 22 February the local authorities committed a fresh act of barbarism by again abducting the children.

'A Volga car drove right up to the school door and during the third lesson the headmaster came into the classroom and called Galya out to the staff-room, where there were the secretary of the Party organisation of the Zhdanov collective farm, V. I. Soltan, and his bodyguard, A. D. Kurash, and, hiding behind a cupboard, the policeman Lebed. The headmaster told Galya that she must return to the children's home, and at that moment the policeman Lebed came out from behind the cupboard and fell upon her. He carried her to the car. She was shouting "Help! Help!", trying to break away with all her might. The policeman fell in the struggle, but didn't release his prey from his arms. And where could

135

the little girl escape to anyway? At the same time our daughter Shura (short for Alexandra—Ed.) was taken out of the class by the doctor's assistant V. M. Mikhalchuk to take some tablets. While she was taking the tablets she was suddenly seized from behind by A. D. Kurash and thrown into the car. The car moved off; the children began to scream; the secretary, V. I. Soltan, covered the children's mouths to drown their screaming, but the violent cries that escaped struck terror to the inhabitants of the village. Besides this, our daughter Shura was sick all the way, and was delivered to the children's home more dead than alive.'

□

The next blow to the family was delivered in November 1968. Mrs Sloboda was arrested, along with her brother and brother-in-law, and sentenced to four years in the labour camps on account of her work in the little church. Her husband was left alone to look after the three younger children, Kolya, Lyusya, and little Pavlik, aged only four. That Christmas the older girls asked permission to go home for the holidays, and were granted it. To their dismay, when they arrived their mother was not there. Their father consoled them, saying, 'Christians who love the Lord much have to follow a difficult path.'

Finally, in February 1970, the three younger children were taken into care leaving the father alone in the house. The most recent report, of October 1972, states that the three youngest are still in a home, while Galya and Shura have been allowed home to their father.

Stories such as this show a system which claims to care deeply for the welfare of its children in a poor light. Yet, strange as it may seem, the educationalists and psychologists have produced plausible justifications for their actions. Religion, they claim, is actually harmful to children—both mentally, morally and even physically. The argument is clearly irrational and based on false premises—no more than a cloak for the unreasoning hostility of the Communist-trained mind for rival ideologies. Wild generalisations are made from preconceptions which have just enough truth in

136

them to be convincing. Here is an example of such reasoning, from I. I. Ogryzko's book *Children and Religion* (Leningrad, 1970):

☐

'Religion suppresses the striving of children towards knowledge, science and culture. Penetrating the childish mind, it kills not only the child's desire for knowledge but his belief in his own ability to gain this knowledge, in his own powers. A teacher of Russian in the 82nd school in Tbilisi, Maria Grigorievna Tryapitsina, had her attention frequently drawn to one of her pupils, Vanya Kozenko. Right through the lessons he would sit, his arms folded, motionless, silent, with an expression of submissiveness and apathy. In his face there was no sign of thought, nor even a smile. This sort of disciplined behaviour was worse than kicking up a row. In a composition entitled *An interesting event in my childhood*, he wrote this: "The most important thing on earth is God. He created everything. His will rules everything. Man should not strive to know or understand everything, but only to believe. Nothing interesting has ever happened to me. When I was five, one of the neighbours took me into her room and began to read a mysterious story from the Bible. The fantastic people in the story talked in a strange way, not straightforward . . . Now I am afraid of the judgement of God." The teacher visited the boy's family. It turned out that their home was a meeting-place for the Baptists. There children would listen to the story of almighty God and the insignificance of sinful man, and would see the sorrow, tears and sighs of prayer. They were forbidden to think for themselves, to express doubts or opinions. This was the source of the boy's cowed attitude, his self-defeat and silence. By accepting belief in God he had lost faith in himself.'

☐

The crude stereotype of the believing child portrayed here is not unusual in atheist literature. There is nothing in literature from the Christian side to indicate that it might be true. Indeed, even official sources often contradict each

137

other. The *Bulletins* of the Baptist Council of Prisoners' Relatives, (nos. 10 and 11, 1972), reproduced some character reports on schoolchildren written by their teachers. Although such critical phrases as 'withdrawn', 'never confides in anyone', do appear, other children are different: 'Larisa reads widely in literature and enjoys English language'—no lack of intellectual liveliness here.

Another criticism the atheists make of the effect of a religious upbringing is that children become socially withdrawn and fail to mix with other children of their own age. Religious values are positively immoral according to the Communist code, because they teach that devotion to God comes before love of one's fellow men. Likewise, the expectation of beatitude in heaven is said to cause neglect of the earthly needs of others. A concern for personal salvation is made out to be over-individualistic, and, above all, incompatible with the Communist morality of the collective. Finally, church activities take children away from 'normal' social life, especially such activities as the Young Pioneers, the Communist boy scouts. A Christian child, say the atheists, will inevitably be morally, psychologically and socially stunted. Here is another reason for the authorities to intervene in his upbringing. Here again is the view of *Children and Religion*:

☐

'The Party teaches children awareness of the collective and mutual aid: one for all and all for one. But religion teaches the believer to care most of all about himself, his own soul: "Lord, give me this", "Lord have mercy", and so on, which nourishes individualism and egoism. Believers do have their own version of the collective, but a religious one. They call their fellow-believers "brothers" and "sisters". But the neighbour who belongs to another religion or none is no "brother" or "sister", but a "lost sheep" or "anti-Christ" and so on. Believing parents may induce in their children this negative attitude to the "sinful world"—the collective which is not incarcerated in a prison of beliefs. The press often reports cases of believing parents forbidding their children to join school organisations of Little Octobrists, Pioneers and Komsomol (Communist Youth organisations—Ed.)

'The Baptist mother Olshevskaya, whose children Nadya and Grisha are pupils of one of the schools in Rostov-on-Don, inculcated into her son such a fear of torments beyond the grave that he tore off his five-pointed star badge and refused to be a Little Octobrist. His sister Nadya took part in the following conversation:

"Do you have any friends, Nadya?"

"Yes."

"Where are they?"

"They are all believers."

"But why do you have no friends at school?"

"They are all anti-Christs." '

□

Once again there is a different story to be told through the character references given to young Baptists. 'Took an active part in the social life of the class and the school. Friendly with members of the pupils' collective,' says one. Yet there is a truth here too. Many children of Christian families must find themselves under psychological stress at school. Even if no direct pressure is put on them to become atheists, they are in the centre of a tug-of-war. Beloved parents tell them one thing, respected adults at school the contrary. Who are they to believe? Small wonder if children sometimes become withdrawn and defensive.

Intellectually incurious and dull, psychologically pathetically inadequate—this is the atheist's stereotype of the believer's child. Finally, some literature asserts that Christianity can even do physical damage. Parents whose minds are so set on heaven that they neglect the temporal needs of their children are one example of this. The Lenten fast, observed in Orthodox families, is said to be harmful to children's health. Then there are examples of babies becoming ill and even dying as a result of being baptised by immersion, as is the Orthodox custom. Finally, a belief that God's will, not their own effort, is the orderer of all things is said to cause believers to fail in proper care for their children. Some have been accused of refusing medical aid on the grounds that 'if God wills, the child will get better'. All these things can be brought against the religious family.

For some Christian families their faith leads to the heartbreak of separation, and, for the parents, the sight of their children being brought up in an alien environment. For the vast majority, however, the centre of the conflict of their way of life with that of their society is the school. Even if they have not first attended kindergarten, from the age of seven the Christian parent must see his or her child going daily to a school where atheism is a subject on the curriculum. Not only this, a keen atheist teacher will do his best to slant every subject to include some antireligious propaganda. In history, the evil effect of religious wars can be described; biology gives an opening for ridiculing the idea of a Creator God; physics and chemistry provide a naturalistic explanation of everything, and experiments can even be done to 'prove' that miracles do not exist. Finally, in the top two years of school, children are taught comparative religion with the emphasis on superstition, backwardness and ignorance as the source of all beliefs; and in the final year there are lessons in the Leninist theory of religion, the relationship of the Church to the Soviet state, the state of religion in the local area and methods of atheist propaganda.

Not only is the theory of propaganda taught, but children are expected to put it into practice. From the earliest years they are supposed to take their knowledge home and 'tell grandma and grandpa about it'. By the final year they may even be sent out on propaganda projects. The atheist magazine *Science and Religion* (no. 7, 1970), reports that pupils from a school in Polotsk had been carrying on atheist education amongst workers in a local meat combine. Other schools in the area were doing similar work in a car repair workshop and a glass factory. This sort of active involvement is calculated to bring about a more conscious commitment to atheism, as well as being a most effective method of ensuring the material is well learnt. For the believer, the choice is between compromise with his faith or rebellion against the school. It is no longer possible to keep quiet and remain unnoticed.

Once a young person leaves secondary school and enters a college of higher education, atheist education becomes even more intense. The intellectual leaders of the new generation must also be leaders in ideological matters. All students attend a compulsory course in 'Bases of Scientific Atheism', which was first introduced in 1959–60. Once again, practical work is expected. Here is the reason why believers maintain that it is practically impossible for a Christian to complete a course of higher education, even if he should first obtain the necessary good character references from his school teachers. Nevertheless some Christians do succeed in doing so. *Science and Religion* (no. 9, 1970), reports such a case:

☐

'A few years ago *Komsomol Truth* reported a very curious fact. It was unexpectedly discovered that one student of the senior year in a certain college was a believer. His comrades asked him, "How can that be? You got *excellent* for the Marxist philosophy exam. How can you believe in these religious tales?" "What's so odd about it?" he replied. "I was asked questions about the views of Marx and Engels. I know very well what they are. But nobody asked me about my own views . . ." '

☐

Not all Christians would be happy with this situation, however. The *Chronicle of the Lithuanian Catholic Church* (No. 5, February 1973) is deeply concerned that students who are made to write essays on atheistic themes against their true convictions may develop a clouded perception of the truth. Without realising it, the *Chronicle* says, they become hypocrites, insincere and lacking in principle—and cease to see any harm in it. The blame is laid squarely on the shoulders of parents who, so that their children may get on in the world, say 'join the Komsomol; just remember not to renounce God in your heart'.

141

Alongside the school, and reinforcing their work, are the youth organisations. Membership of the junior branches, the Little Octobrists and the Pioneers, is almost universal. The Christian child who prefers not to join stands out from his classmates. He avoids involvement in atheist projects, but he also misses out on the hobby circles, the outdoor activities and the camps. The Komsomol, with membership from the age of fourteen, is not nearly as universal. Nevertheless university students claim almost 100 per cent membership. This is another way in which a Christian, whose conscience will not let him identify with the Party, may be excluded from higher education.

The Christian home and the Soviet school, then, by their very nature are in constant conflict. The *Chronicle of the Lithuanian Catholic Church* (no. 7, 1973), publishes a letter from a young mother to the teacher of her child, which expresses in a restrained and dignified way the essence of this conflict. The spirit of this statement is a long, long way from the portrait of the irrational fanatic painted by the atheists in the role of the Christian parent.

☐

'Dear Teacher of my child,

'We are both children of the same Lithuanian nation; we are both bound not only by blood, language, and cultural inheritance, but also by our common concern with the future of our nation. The future of our nation lies in our children. We both look to them with hope, concern and love. I look to my children; you to yours, to mine, and to many others who gather every day in your classroom. The future of our nation depends on what we give these children, how we prepare them for life, and what kind of persons we form of them. Hence the great responsibility for their future rests on our shoulders.

'Conscious of this great responsibility, and understanding well my duties as a parent, I have been trying from the very beginning to instil in my children those principles which would help them all their life to remain honest, decent and resolute persons. These principles I received from my own parents, have tested and confirmed through the experience of a lifetime, mulled over and reasoned out in my own mind, and decided for them in line with my conscience. That which I hold good and necessary I am duty-bound in conscience to hand on to my children also.

'On the other hand, I also have the right to do so. We parents summoned these children to life, we bring them up, clothe them, feed them, and nurse them when they are ill. No one forbids me to dress my children this way or that, no one interferes with my feeding them that food which in my judgement is necessary for my child. Hence no one has the right to forbid me or stop me from handing on to my children those mental and moral principles which it is my conviction are the most necessary for human beings. I know that it is not right to lie, to steal, to cheat or to kill. This conviction I try also to instil in my children. I know that it is good to act decently, to be honest, to love one's neighbour; and I want to instil these principles in my children. I also know that if one wishes to remain an honourable person it is necessary to struggle against one's own weaknesses, vices and temptations from without. For this struggle I prepare my children. From my experience of life I am convinced that such a struggle is most successful when the person feels a responsibility not only in the eyes of human beings, but also in the sight of God; when one is convinced that one's actions and deeds have not only a temporary, transient value, but also an eternal worth; when one obeys not only the law but also the voice of one's conscience. Hence I consider it an essential duty to bring up my children in a religion and I do not want anyone to interfere with this duty of mine. Moreover, you as a teacher agree that parents have a duty to bring up their children . . .

'I am not alone in bringing up my children. I send them from home to school. There I turn them over to you to be educated. However, it is my wish that you carry on my work, and not destroy it. I want you to equip my child's mind with scientific information and to teach him to make use of this information in his life. That, in my opinion, should be the purpose of the school. However, it is very painful to me that you begin to wreck instead of building. Instead of giving scientific information objectively, and the basics of science, you begin to denigrate my convictions and those of my child. You call my beliefs religious superstition, my education compulsion, while considering the atheism you foist on my child by force to be a free and normal thing.

'If you do not respect my convictions, leave them in peace, just as I do not attack or demean yours. Teach my child to read, to write; explain to him the rules of mathematics and the principles of physics; but do not turn these things into a polemic against those principles which I and my child respect. I do not fear objective facts of science, but I do not want you to instil them in a warped and polemical manner, for the sole purpose of instilling in my child an alien world-view. When you attack my beliefs and those of my child, you use not only appropriately distorted class material; you also seek means in extracurricular activities to root out of my child's mind that which I have sown there. Disregarding my wishes, you force him to join the Pioneers and the Komsomol, and atheist groups. You make fun of his beliefs, in the wall newspaper, on bulletin boards, in atheistic evenings and lectures. You force him to answer various questionnaires and force your way into his conscience. And if my child were weaker or if I were unable to steel him in every way, you would cripple him morally, teach him to be hypocritical, to mistrust either his parents or his teachers, and most likely both.

'Will my child then not begin to cast about, will he not then begin to deceive both you and me, will he not then begin to seek questionable pleasures, shallow entertainment, will he not then take a direction which neither you nor I want him to take? Will higher ideals be important to him? Will he be concerned with the future of the nation? With the people's good? Perhaps he will become a common egoist, without higher goals, without higher ideals, concerned only with personal pleasures . . .

'I do not wish to tell you how to do your work. That is

your affair as an educator. Truly, it is not easy to work with young people. To educate a child or young adult, to shape his character, is truly a great responsibility and a difficult task. Therefore, in such work there should be no place or time to wreck what I have already built up. On the contrary, in this matter we must both co-operate, reinforcing the work of one another, working together as closely as possible. This is required of the parent, of the teacher—of us both—this is the duty of the sons of the small Lithuanian nation!

'A parent of one of your pupils.'

□

It is not hard to imagine the suffering of a sensitive child caught between the contrasting atmospheres of home and school, anxious to please and yet unable to do so. It seems that the majority nevertheless survive as Christians, their faith even strengthened by the experience of opposition. Indeed this may often be due to the poor quality of atheist instruction, given in many cases by teachers who themselves have no enthusiasm for the subject. An article in the newspaper *Youth of Estonia* (4 April 1973) gives the impression that most children leave school with little more than a disbelief learned by rote, far from the rational, militant atheism expected of them. The Soviet press frequently carries articles exhorting teachers to pay more attention to the education of the children in their charge. A thoroughly convinced Christian child may well have comparatively little trouble in dismissing ill thought-out and crudely demonstrated proofs of the non-existence of God.

The child who, however, in the course of his schooldays comes up against a keen atheist teacher who is determined to eliminate believing children from his school, will have no easy time. There are more weapons in the atheist arsenal than mere appeals to reason. Teachers are encouraged to engage in 'personal work' with the aim of converting their religious pupils to atheism. Such work may range from gentle persuasion and attempts to involve the child in secular activities, through exposure, mockery and ridicule all the way to threats of lowered academic grades and even

145

expulsion from schools and colleges. There are indeed cases of violence being used against children and of the intervention of the KGB.

It is only fair to the theorists of atheist education to say that they do not recommend violent methods. Some articles have described the use of threats or of ridicule as mistakes: they only serve to confirm the child in the beliefs he is being persecuted for. *Children and Religion* (pp. 129–35) deplores 'administrative' methods, including the removal of children from their parents, and tells a story to illustrate the point:

☐

'The workers in the meat combine in Kostroma knew K. V. Kiseleva to be a conscientious worker. But the trouble was, the factory committee was told, she went to church and took her daughter with her, and would not let her join the Pioneers. How many times they had tried to tell her that God was a delusion and the Church a lot of superstitions! But she refused to take any notice and did not attend lectures. It was decided that the child must be rescued from the mire—after all, there were always the courts and children's homes.

'One need hardly say that such primitive weapons in the fight against the religious beliefs of this woman were of no use. Quite a different approach was used to Kiseleva by her daughter's schoolteacher Solovyova. She frequently visited Kiseleva and came to know all her joys and sorrows, cares and fears. The mother was very distressed by her daughter's lack of success. So she taught her daughter to be religious in the unfeigned hope that the child would become more industrious and make better progress. In such a situation the teacher decided that the way to the woman's heart was through her maternal feelings. When she met Xenia Vasili-evna she praised her daughter Valya for her accuracy and application.

' "But Valya reads very little," added the teacher, "and books are essential to developing her ability. Try to see that she reads."

'Another time the teacher led the conversation to the

subject of the school collective and the Pioneer organisation:

' "There is no point in your forbidding Valya to be a Pioneer. It only upsets her not to be like the other children. It is difficult for her."

' "If it's better for her to be a Pioneer, then let her join."

'The woman's love for her daughter had overcome yet one more superstitition.

'The teacher asked other colleagues to pay more attention to Valya Kiseleva. Gradually her marks improved. The little girl grew happier and came out of herself. The change in her had its effect on her mother. Feeling that a real friend who cared about her was Valya's teacher, she now went for comfort, help and advice not to the church but to the school.

'Soon Kiseleva was seen at the club too. Now she recognised that the lectures concerned herself and sought the answers to her problems in the speakers' words. She found real human relationships with unbelievers.'

□

There are other such success stories in the Soviet press. The gentle approach is not only kinder, it is more effective, the literature claims. Nevertheless in a large number of cases the advice goes unheeded. In practice children meet with various kinds of threats and discrimination. Not only do their teachers bring pressure to bear on them, but classmates are encouraged to help make the Christians conform. An element of every Soviet school's life is the wall newspaper, edited by pupils and pinned up on a notice-board for all to see. Believers may be mocked, caricatured or censured here. Alternatively special class meetings may be held to conduct inquisitions into the lives of children whose conduct is not up to the expected standards—and this includes believers. The whole spirit of the Soviet school lends itself readily to such use. Children are taught that it is their duty to correct those who are going astray. So strongly is the sense of the class collective instilled that the nonconformity of one member is felt to be a stain on the character of all. There are competitions between different schools in conformity to the Soviet ideal; a believer in the class may lead to a loss of chances. Children can be cruel to one another, and serious cases of bullying have been reported where a Christian child is the victim. In 1969, for example, a petition from Baptist mothers—signed by no less than 1,453 of them—was sent to Mr Brezhnev citing many cases of children suffering in Soviet schools. Here is one example from the document: Nina Rudich, a widow from Bobrovitsa in the Chernigov region, has two sons at school:

□

'From the beginning of the school year, the teacher M. I. Cherednichenko forced my younger son Volodya to wear a star (the Little Octobrists' badge). To achieve this she stood him in the corner, or beside his desk in the classroom, first periodically, then every day, saying, "You'll stand there until you wear the star."

'The pupils, encouraged by their teacher's example, started to stand him in the corner before lessons as well. The teacher gave him the nickname "Little Jesus" (and lowered his behaviour mark by four points), which made the pupils hostile to my son. Rejecting the path of reasonable explanation, she deliberately whipped up the whole class, until three of his classmates, V. Menshun, A. Ovodov, and V. Shestun, did a terrible thing. On 19 November 1968 on the way home from school, these children threw my son Volodya on to the roadway under a moving tractor. It was only thanks to the quick reaction of the driver, who braked sharply, that he was not killed.

'But they did not stop at that. They dragged him to the gutter, threw him down in the mud and went on hitting him about the head with their fists and kicking him in the stomach, shouting, "You're disgracing our class because you don't wear a star."

'Now he is unable to go to school, but the doctors pay no attention at all, attempting to present the illness from another angle, making out that he must have tests done in a psychiatric hospital. Indeed, he obviously has a "general trauma of the organism"; but in order to take away responsibility from the teacher, they diagnose it as a general type of cold: "catarrh of the upper respiratory passages", although his throat is perfectly all right and he has no cough. In fact, I told the doctor myself at the very start that it was from a beating. Are our doctors really so incompetent that they cannot distinguish between an illness from a cold and a beating?

'All this was done to cover up for the teacher, who incited the pupils to commit this terrible act.'

☐

Given a victim, some children are not slow to take advantage. Though not all cases are as violent, many Christian children must suffer acutely from the social ostracism they experience.

A child's academic development may be affected too. Low marks may be given for no other reason than that a child is a believer and is known to go to church. *The Chronicle of the Lithuanian Catholic Church* (no. 7, 1973) tells this story from the town of Vabalninkas:

☐

'During another class, Mrs Morkuniene called on Miss Jurganaite to recite. The girl had barely begun to answer, when the teacher interrupted her, saying that she had begun to respond incorrectly. Taking a book, the teacher read the first part and told the girl to continue. When Miss Jurganaite explained that she did not have the book which the teacher had, the latter shot back: "If God loved you, He would chuck the book down from heaven for you, just like that!"

'The girl tried to speak on, but the teacher declared, "God did not save you—you get a two." It was clear to the whole class why the girl received a poor mark.'

☐

The girl mentioned here, the *Chronicle* goes on, was later expelled from technical school. Baptists too may suffer setbacks, as the Council of Prisoners' Relatives' *Bulletin*, no. 11, 1972, explains. It reproduces a composition written by a fifteen-year-old Baptist, Lyudmila Negoda of Kiev, who was given the subject, *What is happiness?* Writing honestly according to her convictions, Lyudmila wrote that the only true happiness lies in loving God and living according to the teachings of Jesus Christ:

□

'Only the Bible tells us how to love truly—it contains the clearest, most unchanging, universally comprehensible and practical teaching on how each person must live. Of all knowledge, the teaching of Christ is the most certain, the most alive. Many people do not want to follow this teaching, because they are afraid of the storm of doubt in their minds that they might have chosen a false way of life. I believe that in following the path laid down by Christ I shall find happiness.'

□

On this forthright statement the teacher's comments are far from sympathetic. It is not what 'we taught you'. 'All the class wrote very well about happiness,' the final note goes, 'but you wrote like an old woman.'

Education in the Soviet Union is compulsory up to the age of fifteen, but after that, children are selected for further education, whether academic or technical. Further education is not universally available, and competition may be fierce. Believers may already be at a disadvantage through low school marks; a further setback can come at the time of the writing of a character report. In spite of the principle of Soviet education, laid down by Lenin himself, that race and creed must be no grounds for discrimination in the field of education, a young person's beliefs are often mentioned in the character reference. These references, provided by the secondary school, form a part of the basis for selection for further education. The Baptist Council of Prisoners' Relatives' *Bulletin* (no. 11, 1972), states that:

□

'In compiling testimonials on children of believing parents the headmaster and teachers of a school refer to the fact that a child belongs to a particular faith and request the place of education to exercise continual control and influence through fellow-students and staff . . .

'Such testimonials are calculated to give information to places of secondary and higher education which may close the door to further study for the student.'

□

Should Christians succeed in reaching higher education and survive the compulsory ideological courses, it is possible that they may still not be able to complete their course of study. Expulsion of believers is not uncommon. The Baptist mothers' letter of 1969 again:

□

'*Expulsion from schools and colleges for faith in God*: this phenomenon has been legalised by you, (Brezhnev—Ed.) since you have not reinstated a single person upon the complaints of those expelled. It has become common practice in all institutes of intermediate and higher education. After preliminary conversations with the believing children, they are told to renounce their faith or be thrown out, they are given a mark of two out of five for social studies and expelled. Your replies to complaints confirm the expulsions.

'In this way A. P. Alexeyev and G. G. Kuznetsov from Kiev were expelled, also Yevdokia Volostrova and her brother Pavel. Veniamin M. Karataev was converted beside his mother's grave on the day of her funeral, after which he was dismissed from the fifth year of a Moscow institute as a believer in God. Ya. Klopot-Makarchuk was expelled from the fourth year of a medical institute for her convictions; there have been many others.'

□

So the Soviet authorities ensure that those who are given the education to reach positions of influence are rarely Christians. What education is available to the believer is not a happy process. The forms of harassment and discrimination are many, and all cannot be catalogued here. From the singling out of a small child by his teacher, to actual physical violence, the spectrum is broad and the permutations many. One final tale, however, may be told. The Baptist Church at Barnaul in southwestern Siberia has been vociferous in its protests at the appalling treatment it has suffered over the years at the hands of the police. Their children have not been exempt: so much so that for eighteen months, from March 1972 to September 1973, they refused to allow their children to attend school. In spite of threats to take the children away, they held out until, in July 1973, guarantees were given by the authorities that their children would be treated better. The chief complaint was that children were constantly being interrogated about their Church activities and those of their parents. The real instigators, it seems, were the local KGB. Hence the events cannot really be seen as a consequence of the Soviet educational system. Rather they are a further example of the way in which it can be used as an instrument of the State in a campaign against local believers.

In March 1972 ninety Baptist parents from Barnaul wrote to the United Nations:

☐

'Particularly in recent times our children have been undergoing cruel outrages in their schools, not only from their fellow pupils but from representatives of the authorities, who carry out forcible interrogations at the schools. The most recent interrogation was carried out by Investigator Shtyryov on 16 March 1972. The interrogation of the children was carried out in the absence of their parents. In order to make the child go into the office for questioning, violence was used. One small boy was pushed head over heels down a staircase. Unable to bear the thought of the interrogation, terrified, the boy ran away and hid in the lavatory. A second interrogation was carried out by Shtyryov of another child in class, in the presence of all the pupils, during a lesson. From this it is possible to conclude what attitude his comrades will have towards this child of a believing family. Fearing for the physical well-being of our children, since all these deplorable acts are having an adverse effect on their health, we, their parents, are obliged not to allow our children to attend school classes. In sending our children to school we want them to acquire knowledge, not to be made into cripples. The results of previous similar events clearly indicate this may be the case, when children are left with stutters or weak hearts from dreadful experiences and sheer terror which they have never known in their own homes. Thus, since 16 March our children have not been to school. Their parents are already to be ordered to pay fresh fines, it is said in the schools.'

□

Another letter, of September 1972, gives further details of the unfortunate children's experiences:

□

'Since March 1972 our children have not been attending school, a fact about which we have written many times to various people. We parents do not send our children to school so that they can be maltreated, but so that they can receive knowledge. How are our children actually treated at school? Here are some examples: a physics teacher at the 51st school, Zoya Mikhailovna, in the middle of her lessons slanderously insulted believers whose children were present. Investigators Rylov, Shtyryov and others with the support of the teachers were so rough when interrogating our children that the frightened children could not reply. And how could they answer such questions as, "Do you believe in God? Who taught you to believe? Do you pray? Where did you see God? Do you go to church? Where do you meet? Who leads the services? Who preaches? What do they preach about? Is there a Sunday-school? Who teaches the children? How many children go to church? Whose children? Who runs the children's meeting? What kind of programme of lessons is there for the children?" and so on.

'If the investigating authorities were able to get anything out of the children in this way, it would be enough to put a believer in prison for three to five years. During trials they try to make children give evidence against believers. As well as this, children are put under arc lights, cameras, television cameras and suchlike. Then a leading article will appear in the paper describing how "believers tried to escape trial, but were exposed, and got what they deserved". After such "atheist remedies", some of our children have become ill and started to stutter.

'The above facts represent a part of the sufferings our children have recently gone through. When all these outrages cease and we are given a guarantee of our children's future safety, they will go back to school.'

☐

The children eventually returned to school, and no further outrages have been reported.

The experience of the Barnaul children is not unique. Even those who escape such extremes will not find that the Soviet school treats the Christian with much kindness, whatever the educationalists may say to the contrary. The constant battering of the mind with atheist propaganda; the stigma and the ridicule; the frustration of academic potential unfulfilled—none of these are easy for the young mind to bear. Nevertheless the picture is not so bleak that the outcome may not be encouraging. Young Christians learn early that the pathway of belief is not to be an easy one, and if their faith is not broken it can only be toughened. The training of the Soviet school is a necessary one if young Christians are to keep the faith in a wider community as they grow up. Many of them will. Let a young Baptist girl, who wrote to the Council of Prisoners' Relatives' *Bulletin* (no. 11, 1972), have the last word:

☐

'At school there is pressure on us—there are three girls and myself, and I am several years older than the others. One day, it was in 1971, my friend Lyusya, who used to wear a Pioneer scarf, and is from a believing family, gave up wearing it. I went with her to the prayer-meetings and to the youth meeting and somehow the teacher got to know and began to put pressure on me, although they had already questioned me thoroughly. Now they began saying: 'You live an unenlightened life yourself, you don't go to the cinema, nor to the theatre—but where are you dragging her?' One day she began questioning me even in class in front of

154

the others, for almost a whole lesson. But I did not get upset
—on the contrary, my spirit rose up in me and I prayed, and
so with Christ I overcame the enemy.'

'I believe, Lord, and confess that You send the fire of testing so that we may emerge from it pure, transformed and prepared for the re-fashioning of our lives!

'I believe, Lord, that the world is shaken so that all peoples, hearing Your word and receiving it, may be united in one loving family obedient to Your law!

'I believe, Lord, that in the midst of the storms and heat You shelter us under the wings of Your limitless mercy, and lead us through the Golgotha of expiation to Your indescribable light!

'Your ways are inexpressible, Lord! You alone command when the cup of suffering shall be drunk to the end and when the bright day of our resurrection shall dawn. Your will be done!

'I believe, Lord, and I confess that each effort of ours to live according to the truth and in true faith in Your great wisdom will hasten the time for the resurrection of all men and prepare the way for Your coming.

'Consciously and hour by hour I want to participate in the redemption of the world, to remain steadfast in the midst of upheavals so that I may be one of Your lights in the world!

'Lord, I go into the world to do Your will and with one desire only—to remain a faithful servant in the place where You send me.

'Amen.'

Some further titles in Lakeland Paperbacks

I FOUND GOD IN SOVIET RUSSIA
John Noble   no. 161

> Through the witness of his fellow prisoners in Soviet
> labour camps the author, an American citizen, was
> brought to belief in Christ.

TORTURED FOR HIS FAITH
Haralan Popov   no. 183

> The stirring testimony of a Bulgarian pastor, imprisoned
> for thirteen years for preaching the Christian gospel.

FORGIVE ME, NATASHA
Sergei Kourdakov   no. 301

> A young Russian police officer's own story of his
> brutal persecution of Christians, and of his search
> for their God.

CZECH MATE
David Hathaway   no. 311

> Over the years a British pastor took 150,000 Bibles and
> Testaments behind the Iron Curtain. Then he was
> arrested and imprisoned in Czechoslovakia.

THE BOOK THEY COULDN'T BAN
André Morea   no. 337

> For several years the author of this remarkable book,
> a government employee under a communist administra-
> tion, secretly visited groups of Christians in his own
> country, preaching and distributing Bibles.